MIXED METHODS

MIXED METHODS

A short guide to
applied mixed methods research

SAM LADNER, PhD

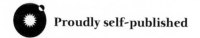 Proudly self-published

ISBN 978-1-7342178-0-3

Icons by Smashicons

CONTENTS

LIST OF TABLES AND FIGURES

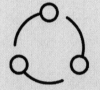

UNDERSTANDING THE QUAL/QUANT TRADE-OFF

I ONCE ATTENDED A PRESENTATION on a very large study about Chinese innovation practices, involving many thousands of Chinese businesses and their economic output data. The slides were full of charts and graphs and, I clearly recall, a very small font. But what was that study really about? Who were these companies? What was important to them? How might they react to challenges? How exactly did they innovate? I couldn't tell you. All I remember is that "China is big." This study had no characters, no plot, and no story. I cannot remember really anything about this study, even though it clearly was thorough, because it lacked the qualitative detail we humans love.

Humans are much better able to recall the rich qualitative details in stories about people. We tell stories constantly. It is the primary way we make sense of the world. Neuroscientists tell us that stories underpin the basic neurological processes of human understanding (Yuan, Major-Girardin, & Brown, 2018). The narrative arc and a focus on characters give the human mind a coherent picture, easily understood, recalled, and shared. For applied researchers, it has the added benefit of putting people in their customer's shoes.

Stories starring a customer (and not the CEO) have a way of eliciting what ethnographers call the "emic" position, or what business people would call customer obsession. Isn't it odd, then, that we don't use this universal way of sharing knowledge when we share knowledge about customers? Sadly, stories don't provide what many believe to be essential for research: the scale of any incidence or why something causes something else.

For millennia, humans told stories to understand the world. But it wasn't until the advent of science that we began to understand even the simplest of root causes. Why do apples fall from trees? It isn't because a hungry monster lives under the tree and forces the apple to the ground with its magic—it is because of gravity. How did the massive stone statues of Easter Island get placed around the island, before the invention of cranes or trucks? Ancient stories about these enigmatic statues say they "walked" out of the quarries and into places of honor. That's partly true, according to some archaeologists, who published results from an experiment using the technology available at the time. Using ropes and people, these researchers were able to make a replica statue rock back and forth and "walk" (Lipo, Hunt, & Haoa, 2013). Maybe the stories *and* the science are both right. Stories and science give us different things.

Scientific inquiry—or the methodical, systematic and objective development of knowledge—is what underpins our ability to live in the world the way we do. Science gave us the ability to fly, to communicate worldwide instantaneously, to heat our homes safely, to survive reliably past early childhood or through serious illness, to listen to music at any time, to capture beautiful moments forever, and, perhaps most importantly, the ability to access any of this knowledge from anywhere, at any time. It is science that has allowed the human race to flourish. Even on Earth, the most hospitable of planets, this is a feat of survival and ingenuity. Knowing how often something happens and why it happens is the gift of science. This gift has kept us alive.

Scale and causation are appropriately quantitative in nature. Yet—as I learned listening to that presentation on Chinese innovation—it takes an extraordinary amount of work for a human to make sense of quant data. How did the participants of that Chinese study feel about their companies? How did their employees cope with unexpected problems? How does a community move 4.35 metric tons of stone? Quant research stops short of this. Quantitative researchers focus on scale on causation but fail to provide coherence and participant focus. Qualitative research, by contrast, focuses on coherence and participant focus but lacks scale and causation. How often do innovation strategies fail? What precisely causes a statue to move, and how much force is needed? Qual researchers avoid these questions. When we use quant data, we put the sensemaking onus on the consumer of the research, and when we use qual data, we sacrifice scale and causation. This is a terrible trade-off.

However, you do not have to choose between coherence and participant focus on the one hand, and scale and causation on the other. You can have both if you mix research methods. This short book[1] stems from the belief that this artificial separation between qualitative and quantitative research can

---

[1] And by short, I mean SHORT! If you are reading this as a sample, you should know this book runs a very tight 20,000 words. Calling this a book doesn't do justice to all the other books out there (including my own book, Practical Ethnography, which runs a verbose 65,000 words).

and should be bridged, particularly in an applied setting. This is a challenging thing to do, not just because of practical concerns, but also because of fundamental differences between qual and quant researchers' techniques, processes, training, and most importantly, philosophical perspectives. Mixed methods research can fail for practical reasons, but more often than not, it fails because the researchers themselves fail to appreciate the deeper implications of mixing philosophical traditions.

In this book, I will describe what mixing methods is all about, and why it is so difficult to achieve. I am an applied researcher, working in technology and focusing mostly on ethnography as a method. Any ethnographer will tell you that they trade in stories. How did my participant get to work today? What were the concerns she had when she changed jobs? Why did she decide to remodel her kitchen? In my book, *Practical Ethnography* (Ladner, 2014), I explain that stories are the way to learn what participants value, and for researchers to gain the emic perspective (that is, to focus on what the participants consider important, not what the researcher, the product manager, or even the CEO thinks is important). Ethnographers spend much of their time collecting stories from their participants (note how I did not use the word anecdote here; see more about anecdotes below).

Why you should banish the word "anecdote" from your research practice

I purposefully did not use the word "anecdote" for two reasons. First, it is not an accurate representation of what qualitative research actually is. Anecdotes lack method. They are not collected in any particular way, but simply told, heard and passed along without regard for systematic, methodical, or reproducible results. Qualitative data, on the other hand, includes stories that are collected in consistent ways across contexts, participants and researchers. Qualitative data (which includes stories) are collected, analyzed and summarized thoughtfully; anecdotes are tossed off in casual conversation. The two simply are not equivalent. The second reason I do not use the word anecdote is because of the dreaded phrase "anecdotal evidence." Qualitative researchers the world over groan at this phrase because it connotes a lack of validity. Qualitative data has many tests for validity that mere anecdotes do not. Yet, by calling a story an "anecdote," a person is undermining this story's ability to represent the true, real and rich experience of any individual.

Stories are core to the ethnographic endeavor (Narayan, 2012). They are the vehicle for "thick description" that Clifford Geertz considers the core of culture itself (Geertz, 2000). Telling stories is how you cohere thick description. Your participants become real, intelligible, sympathetic, and the protagonist in whatever it is your organization is doing. No longer a bit-player, the customer takes center stage in qual research.

Sadly, however, ethnographers and non-ethnographers alike often believe ethnographic data to be solely qualitative. Those who practice ethnography will often resist quantification, thinking it sullies the nature of their data. Non-ethnographers may dismiss ethnography altogether, believing it to lack predictive power, which they take to be the sole purpose of research. In other words, some falsely believe that ethnography can provide coherence and participant focus but cannot provide scale or causation. Many ethnographers themselves have rejected this artificial line (e.g., Anderson, Nafus, Rattenbury, & Aipperspach, 2009; Denzin & Lincoln, 2000; Lecompte & Shensul, 1999), yet this separation often remains in practice.

This book started as a webinar I gave to the Ethnographic Praxis in Industry Conference (EPIC) community in March 2019.[2] If you are a current academic, this book will not be for you; it is short, by design. If you are looking for a treatise on mixed methods, this ain't it. I'd recommend finding a more academic work such as Mario Luis Small's excellent summary "How To Conduct A Mixed Methods Study," which I draw from heavily (Small, 2011), or Creswell's classic book *Research Design:*

---

[2] The webinar itself was recorded. Members of the EPIC community can watch this video, which includes my lecture and accompanying slides, on the EPIC web site http://epicpeople.org

Qualitative and Quantitative Approaches (J. W. Cresswell, 1994), or his work *Designing and Conducting Mixed Methods Research* co-authored with Ann Carroll Klassen, Vicki Plano Clark, and Katherine Clegg Smith (2007), or his short paper focusing on health research specifically (J. Cresswell, Klassen, Plano Clark, & Clegg Smith, 2011). This book is an introduction to the topic, with some practical guidance on how to manage the pitfalls of mixing methods in applied settings. It is for applying research methods in a corporate setting, and will help applied researchers who have gaps in their methods training.

I am writing this book primarily for the people in my EPIC webinar who asked for a written companion to the presentation, but also for the many applied researchers working in marketing, communications, health care, technology, financial services, and other industries who have asked my advice about how to mix methods effectively. Students currently studying qualitative research methods or even data science will likely get value from this book, particularly if they are planning a mixed methods study.

This book augments some of my earlier writing on applied research methods. In my own work, I realized there is a distinct lack of good sources for applied research methods. Academic books are a must-read for any applied researcher, but there is an additional set of questions that academic books cannot answer. For example, ethnography can be practiced in the private sector, but I learned there were no definitive sources on how to do that. So I wrote *Practical Ethnography* (Ladner, 2014) to help applied researchers adapt the original method and bring it into the applied setting. I also noticed that project management is a key competency for applied researchers, yet there were few academic sources to help them learn how to do that. So I wrote "Managing

The Private Sector Research Project" in the *Sage Handbook of Research Management* (Ladner, 2015) to outline the key, and distinct, concerns that applied researchers must consider when managing their research.

This book on mixed methods comes from a similar discovery about mixing methods in the applied setting. Applied researchers can choose from literally thousands of books on applied quantitative research. There are far fewer (but still a large number) of applied qualitative research books as well. Yet, there is a distinct gap in applied mixed methods research. Writing this book fills that gap. It is a selfish endeavor, frankly, because it gives me a chance to explore my own craft in a deeper way. I want to share that journey with others. I want you to carve out some time, luxuriate in just thinking about research methods, and discover new things about your own practice. Put your feet up and find a quiet place to read. Come with me and explore mixed methods.

A MIXED-METHODS EXAMPLE: STORIES AS A NETWORK

LET ME START WITH AN example of a mixed methods study that illustrates the richness a mixed approach can provide. Researchers Bearman and Stovel (2000) set out to answer a sadly all-too-relevant question: how does one become a Nazi? They decided to understand this process by analyzing coming-of-age stories that young Nazis themselves had written. The researchers had a unique data set of stories from an essay contest in the 1930s, which invited people to describe their journey to becoming a Nazi. Six hundred young Nazis submitted their life stories to the contest. This valuable cache of stories reveals much about how a person makes sense of adopting a hateful ideology. If these researchers had stuck to a typical qualitative approach, they might have simply analyzed the stories for themes and reported those themes back. But instead, they chose both qualitative and quantitative methods.

Qualitatively, they focused on the content of the stories themselves. They used narrative analysis, a research method that dissects stories and focuses less on what happened and more on how individuals come to make sense of what happened (Bryman

& Teevan, 2005). Narrative analysis reveals the invisible and subjective process whereby humans understand and synthesize disparate events, settings and people, instead of just the empirical facts of the events themselves. Narrative analysis revealed the process by which people came to understand their new identities as Nazis. But the researchers wanted to learn more: the elements of a narrative (events, settings, people) could provide more insight into this process. This was inspiration for a truly unique mixed methods research study.

Quantitatively, Bearman and Stovel augmented narrative analysis by the more mathematical approach of social network analysis. They used the elements of the narrative and transformed and mapped these elements into a network. They then mathematically analyzed how story elements such as events, settings and people were connected, just as you might analyze a social network. They counted events, settings, and people, and showed how they were connected (if at all) and how far apart these elements were. Just as a social network analyst might measure the distance between any two people in a network, Bearman and Stovel measured the distance between events, settings and people within these Nazi narratives. They discovered a distinct pattern: becoming a Nazi demonstrated a tightly knotted network of these elements, close in time and meaning, while *being* a Nazi was characterized by a series of relatively unrelated events, people and settings. As noted in Figure 1 below, they produced a map of the story elements as a network.

From these two very different methods, they concluded that *becoming* was a distinct phase, and it was a progressive alienation from institutions such as work and school, filled with instances of moving around, and other instances of meeting Nazis. Taken together, these instances numerically suggested a pattern. The degree of interconnectedness of these elements as a network led Bearman and Stovel to conclude,

> In the *becoming* story, cognitions are almost equally likely to send ties [to other story elements] as to receive them [from other story elements], while in the being story, cognitions are almost always the consequence of a prior element. Substantively, this reveals that cognitions play a crucial role in motivating the narrative of becoming... Being a Nazi induces the absence of self-reflexivity (Bearman & Stovel, 2000, pp. 84–85).

This insight suggests that once one becomes a Nazi, they no longer work hard to make sense of their experiences, or to reflect on what they are doing. You can see, then, how important it is to identify the pattern of radicalization before it takes firm root, because once it does, it's very difficult to unwind.

FIGURE 1: *Nazi Life Stories as Networks from Bearman and Stovel*

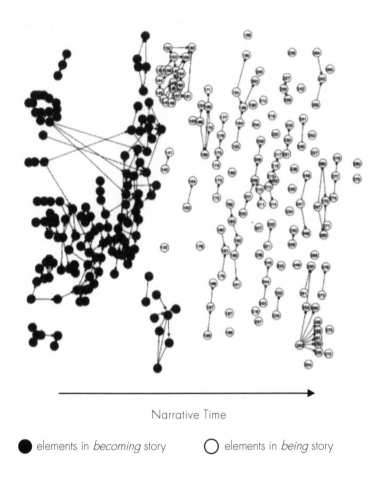

Narrative Time

● elements in *becoming* story   ○ elements in *being* story

At first glance, this unique mixed methods approach offers an intriguing or even slightly confusing new analysis of life narratives. However, upon a closer reading, the research reveals the key aspects to mixing methods: using mathematical methods to explore what are essentially qualitative concepts provides an opportunity for deeper understanding. Methodologists such as Bryman (2006) would call this "complementarity" or the "elaboration, enhancement, illustration, clarification of the results, from one method with the results from another" (Bryman, 2006, p. 105). Instead of just finding the major themes of the narratives, Bearman and Stovel also found how these themes were interconnected mathematically. One can imagine how using qualitative analysis alone might reveal the themes being alienated from church or school, for example. However, it's unlikely it would reveal the tight knotting of this experience with other experiences like moving around or meeting other Nazis, or the fact that this tight knotting falls off after one has transformed into being a Nazi.

This mixed method study shows us that stopping the spread of a hateful ideology hinges on two aspects. First, alienation begins with disconnection from church or school, and with moving around. Second, this study shows that intervening is best done in the becoming phase. Once a person "is" a Nazi, they are no longer reflecting on their lives, making it much harder for them to question their identity. This mixed insight is far richer than just a quant or qual study alone. These researchers provided both scale and causation and coherence and participant focus.

At the same time, these researchers also adopted the extra burden of doing both qualitative and quantitative methods well. Mixing methods provides new opportunities, but also requires new responsibilities.

WHAT ARE MIXED METHODS: MIXING OBJECTIVISM AND CONSTRUCTIVISM

SURPRISINGLY, THERE IS NO AGREED-upon definition of what constitutes a "mixed method" study. Some researchers use the term to indicate that they are using formal mathematical procedures on their data, whatever their form. Others use the word "qualitative" simply to indicate that it is a small sample size alone (Small, 2011). Mixing usually connotes using a combination of qualitative and quantitative methods and data. Quant data are numbers and qual data are qualities, or descriptions, of a thing. As Small notes, this is not universally understood by researchers and non-researchers alike.

In a rather confusing Twitter exchange I had recently, I encountered a designer who used the word "qualitative" to indicate anything that was not verifiably observed using objective observation. After much back-and-forthing, I discovered this designer believed that anything describing subjective perceptions or beliefs was qualitative, even if it is clearly using numbers! In fact, this designer was conflating the word "empirical," or the act of observing something, with the word "quantitative," or numerical data. The word empirical simply refers to direct observation, so quant data can be subjective or empirical, and qual data can be either subjective or empirical.

Ethnographers are typically known for their empirical rigor, by reporting exactly what happens with the eye of both a camera (Crabtree, Rodden, Tolmie, & Button, 2009) and an informed human instrument (Ader, 2011). The difference between empirical and subjective or perceived qualities and quantities are laid out in Figure 2 below.

FIGURE 2: Empirical and Perception-based Qualitative and Quantitative Research

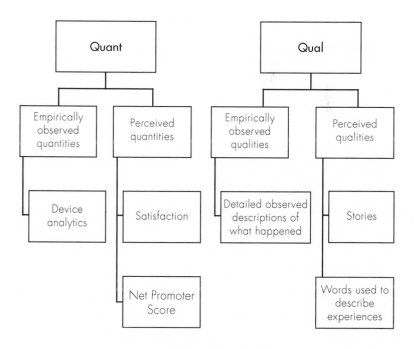

This Twitter exchange surprised me because I clearly underestimated how few people working in applied research have a firm understanding of why and how qual and quant research differ—perhaps because it's not obvious. Cresswell and Plano Clark note that the main differences in qual and quant research are their philosophical assumptions: these assumptions define the word, "methodology" itself. We all have schools of thought about our professional craft, and researchers are no exception. They too have implicit beliefs about their work. Mixing those beliefs is what mixing methods is about:

> Mixed methods research is a research design with philosophical assumptions as well as methods of inquiry. As a methodology, it involves philosophical assumptions that guide the direction of the collection and analysis of data and the mixture of qualitative and quantitative approaches in many phases of the research process (J. W. Cresswell & Plano Clark, 2007, p. 5).

It's helpful here to review the essential characteristics of qualitative and quantitative research, to provide more insight into why describing mixed methods is so very difficult. At their core, these two approaches have differing belief systems about how knowledge is created (epistemology) and even more fundamentally, about what is reality itself (ontology). The epistemological and ontological divide underneath qual and quant methods is what drives our collective hand-wringing, because this is not simply about mixing methods, but about opposing views on reality. If that sounds heavy, it is. That's why we fail to mix methods—because we are using fundamentally different assumptions about what is even real!

As summarized in Table 1, quantitative research begins with the assumption that reality is a stable, objective thing that can be understood and observed. If you have this assumption, it makes sense that you use the scientific method when you create new knowledge. Objectivists tend to adopt what methodologists call "positivism,"[3] or the belief that the human world is just as discoverable through observations as the natural world is. The hallmark of the scientific (positivist) method is *falsifiability*, or the ability to prove an assertion wrong, according to science philosopher Karl Popper (1962). Facts like how many people drive to work and how many mushrooms grow at a given temperature are typical outputs of the positivist method. You can demonstrably show that more than 20 people drive to work on any given day, or that more mushrooms grow best at 18°C.

[3] I find it ironic that the founder of positivism was August Comte, the first sociologist. Comte himself actually rejected the belief that true causation could be established in the study of social life; it was only well into the 20th century that social scientists attempted to claim causation in social research. It turns out human behavior rarely falls neatly into causal models, even if some social scientists tend to argue it does (economists come to mind as an example). Hammersley (2014) notes that "causation" is often understood not as what causes what, but more akin to deep understanding of a complete process. The philosophy of human experience is not as cut-and-dried as many of us believe it to be. Interestingly, neither is *natural science*, as quantum researchers could tell you. Those interested in the philosophical and historical context of this debate can read *The Limits of Social Science: Causal Explanation and Value Relevance* by Martyn Hammersley (Hammersley, 2014).

Hypotheses must be falsifiable. Taking falsifiability into social research is still somewhat controversial in social science circles because firmly establishing causation is much more difficult when studying humans than when studying mushrooms. Irrespective of this challenge, some positivist social scientists argue that causation is the primary goal of social research (Hammersley, 2014).

TABLE 1: Ontology and Epistemology of Qual and Quant Research

	Role of theory in research	Ontological orientation	Epistemological orientation
Quantitative	Deductive, testing of theory	Objectivism	Natural science model / positivism
Qualitative	Inductive, generating theory	Constructionism	Interpretivism

In contrast to objectivist quant researchers, qualitative researchers typically believe that our social reality is *constructed*, which means the human world is not "real" in an objective sense, but based on everyday interpretations humans make when they go about their business. Unlike the natural science model, the constructivist perspective seeks knowledge by focusing on the interpretations humans make. Constructivists explain the social world through this interpretivist approach. It is only through repeated social experience, or what sociologists Berger and

Luckman call "reification," that we come to believe that the social world is as stable as the natural world. Social experiences become firmed into social institutions and we begin to see them as we might see natural phenomena. In their classic book, *The Social Construction of Reality*, Berger and Luckman describe this process: "Through reifications, the world of institutions appears to merge with the world of nature" (Berger & Luckman, 1966, p. 90). At the core, constructivists argue that social reality is not natural; it is created by humans.

In the movie *The Matrix*, this is the view that Morpheus is trying to show young Neo. The world, as Neo knows it, is not "real," but a vast simulation created by machines intent on fooling the entire human race into willingly generating energy for the machines. Morpheus tells Neo everything he believes lacks substance, but he cautions that questioning reality is too existentially troubling for some people:

> The Matrix is a system, Neo. That system is our enemy. But when you're inside, you look around, what do you see? Businessmen, teachers, lawyers, carpenters. The very minds of the people we are trying to save. But until we do, these people are still a part of that system and that makes them our enemy. You have to understand, most of these people are not ready to be unplugged. And many of them are so inured, so hopelessly dependent on the system, that they will fight to protect it. *The Matrix*, 1999

Neo comes to learn, as other constructivists do, that social reality can be bent. Social rules are not fixed, but subject to change and reinterpretation. The goal of constructivist ontology is to understand the process by which people understand their social reality. In Neo's case, reality is a layer of software running over the human hardware. In constructivist social science, reality is a layer of social structures like race, gender, sexual orientation, economic class, or religion.

An illustrative example of this approach is the constructivist analysis of sex and gender. Objectivists believe a person's "sex" is a biological trait, indicated by clearly observable sex characteristics such as facial hair. A man is someone who can grow a beard; a woman is someone who cannot. Case closed. But constructivists point out that there are edge cases of sex characteristics like hormone levels, which trouble this static view.[4] Some women have hormone levels more similar to those of men, yet appear and are accepted as women. They are women for all intents and purposes.

Gender, unlike sex, is a socially defined concept that does not rest on effectively invisible hormone levels, but on social interaction. For this reason, constructivists use the term gender instead of sex because it emphasizes this social negotiation process. Constructivists believe humans "create" their reality through their interpretive lenses such as gender, age, familial ties, racial identity and economic class as shorthand to alleviate

[4] Note that this short book will not discuss this deep and fraught topic in detail. Should you want to learn more about the constructivist perspective of gender, consider carving out about 5-8 years of time, and read all of *Gender Trouble* by Judith Butler. Then perhaps binge-watch all the episodes of *Transparent*, and all episodes of *RuPaul's Drag Race*. You may have a clearer view in about 9-10 years.

the overwhelming cognitive load of everyday living. Social structures like gender are a way to make social interactions smoother and more predictable. If you know someone is a woman, you know how to interact with her, what is expected, and what is not. In the words of Berger and Luckman, social structures alleviate us from making "all those decisions" about how to interact with other humans (Berger & Luckman, 1966).

A CONSTRUCTIVIST VIEW OF TECHNOLOGY

A constructivist perspective I use in my work in technology is the social construction of technology (SCOT) tradition, which sees technology as necessarily shaped by the humans who make and use it. In their early article on the SCOT approach, Pinch and Bijker (1984) argue that technology is inextricably tied to the social context in which it is produced. Designers have intentions that they imprint on the technology. In turn, the users add their interpretations of what the technology is through their usage. This is the concept of "interpretive flexibility," or the fact "that there is flexibility in how people think of, or interpret, artefacts, but also that there is flexibility in how artefacts are *designed*" (Pinch & Bijker, 1984, p. 421, emphasis in original).

The SCOT approach would explain why Facebook, for example, continues to fail to protect its users' privacy: its entire business model is based on selling users' data to advertisers. It also explains why people continue to use Facebook to connect to their friends and families, despite these continued privacy lapses. Interpretive flexibility is why users hack or mod their tools in ways their designers never intended, and it is why usability testing alone does not reveal the full picture of how technology will get adopted.

You can see how this constructivist stance dictates a very different approach to data collection and by extension, the production of knowledge itself. Objectivist researchers may observe "technology use" and take it for granted that people want to complete tasks more quickly. But constructivists may begin to ask, "How do humans interpret this technology?" Data collection for objectivists is straightforward and deductive: did this finding confirm or deny my previously held belief? But for constructivists, inductive approaches are more familiar. What do these humans think this tool is, metaphorically? What do my participants believe about productivity or getting things done? How do they grapple with getting things done faster, but then having more things to do? How does their experience trouble our belief that being faster is always better?

These two ontological orientations lay bare the deep divide: mixed methods research is not simply about mixing data sets—it's about mixing philosophical points of view. This is the underlying reason why you personally might have experienced some unexpected pain in collaborating with other researchers "across the pond," as it were. Yes, you are mixing stories, photos and videos with quantitative summaries such as average age, for example. But you're also mixing expectations, beliefs and even different people. We are trained differently, depending on where we come from. So, if you've experienced this pain, it may be comforting to know that it's not a personal failing but more of a symptom of this philosophical divide.

HOW THE QUAL/QUANT DIVIDE PLAYS OUT

Given these underlying differences in thinking and belief, this qual/quant divide manifests itself in several ways. First, from a procedural perspective, the two approaches have vastly different ways of conducting research. Quantitative researchers focus more on scale and causation, and like to have replicability and precise measurement. This differs significantly from qualitative researchers, who concern themselves with describing richness of context, the nature of change, and having empathy for participants. Qual researchers welcome changes in research design, even after research has begun, because it further demonstrates the empathic, participant-led mindset. Quant researchers, by contrast, spend a lot of time preparing exactly the right research design, and do not deviate from that plan when collecting data because it would introduce confounding variables to their experiments.

The second way this divide manifests is perhaps more important: these two approaches have very different expectations about what constitutes "success." Quantitative researchers expect their results to show the scale of a thing and the nature of its cause. They are disappointed if their results lack this numerical precision, but don't mind if it fails to yield rich stories. Qualitative researchers, by contrast, are disappointed if their results do not yield a coherent explanation of exactly how and in what ways a thing happens, who plays what role, and what kinds of objects are recruited for or rejected from a given process. They expect to spend quality time with their participants and are comfortable with ambiguity. They want their data to yield great stories, with lots of color and details, and they want a complete, coherent understanding.

You can see how success in one approach will look a lot like failure in the other.

Most people working in companies today are unfamiliar with constructivist approaches, so they unfortunately ask for—and usually get—only objectivist-driven data. Yet they hunger for the deep insight of constructivist data. Stakeholders consider scale and causation the only acceptable outcome for any sort of research, but this is only because they are unfamiliar with qualitative concepts of validity. It never fails to surprise me how objections to ethnography's lack of scale and causation just disappear when stakeholders hear great stories, told in detail, with coherence and a focus on customers. It is liberating to simply learn more about how people think, without a narrow focus on "proving" the effects of a single variable. I tell my stakeholders that they have my permission to "luxuriate in the customer" with this kind of research. You can almost see them visibly relax when you give them permission to let go of their unconsciously held objectivist ontology. If they stop focusing solely on scale and causation, and focus instead on coherence and customers, they begin to feel better equipped to make decisions about their products or services. However, most people are simply unaware that there is a qualitative, inductive logic that is just as legitimate as a quantitative, deductive method.

ABANDONING THE SCIENTIC METHOD: THE CREATIVE ENCOUNTER

The scientific method is deductive, and it's what most non-researchers learn in their education in other disciplines such as engineering, marketing, psychology, human resources and business. Unfortunately, as science scholar Carol Steiner writes, the scientific method constrains creative thought. In her analysis of innovative and creative researchers, Steiner finds that the most innovative researchers take a leap away from deductive reasoning: "Losing faith in 'scientific method' has allowed them to understand themselves as other than knowledge-*makers*. Consequently, they often project an openness that allows a different world to shine through for them, the public world" (Steiner, 1999, p. 594, emphasis in original). In their famous ethnographic study of scientists at work, Latour and Woolgar (1979) discovered that even lab-based science rarely conforms to the scientific ideal; it turns out that scientists do not "do science" in a way most of us might recognize (see below). Just like producing art, producing knowledge is a chaotic and messy process.

Losing faith in the scientific method is quite freeing when you are in the early stages of trying to understand something. Existentialist psychotherapist Rollo May calls this experience "the encounter," or the act of falling in love with your subject matter, without regard for specific outcomes. The encounter, in May's view, is key to both art *and* science. Artists and scientists alike must abandon procedure and simply soak up their subject:

Artists encounter the landscape they propose to paint — they look at it, observe it from this angle and that. They are, as we say, absorbed in it. Or, in the case of abstract painters, the encounter may be with an idea, an inner vision, that in turn may be led off by the brilliant colors on the palette or the inviting rough whiteness of the canvas. The paint, the canvas, and the other material then become a secondary part of this encounter; they are the language of it, the *media*, as we rightly put it. Or scientists confront their experiment, the laboratory task, in a similar situation of encounter. (May, 1994, p. 39).

It is this same liberation my stakeholders exhibit when I tell them to fall in love with their customer. It is a mindset that is open, exploratory, curious, and even a little excited.

Laboratory Life and the manufacturing of scientific facts

In their study of the scientific work at the Salk Institute, Latour and Woolgar (1979) found that even at this world-famous lab, few researchers actually engaged in true deductive logic. Scientific facts were "manufactured" in the lab, they argued, through a complex social process that hinged upon the promulgation of data through instrument readouts and writing of scientific papers. They observed many moments of inductive reasoning, which the scientists themselves later retrofitted into a deductive frame when writing up a paper. Laboratory Life reveals that deduction and induction are both part of even the most "scientific" practice.

Designers may recognize this process as similar to the "double diamond," or the continuous process of divergence and convergence that exemplifies the design process in general (The British Design Council, 2015). Designers typically begin projects by exploring widely, but they must also master the ability to converge onto a single idea, whether it's the specific problem they are trying to solve, or the solution they are trying to craft. This process is similar to the research design process, which also requires divergence in the early stages to gather thick description of the context and the actors, and then convergence once the researcher begins to focus on scale and causation. Designers develop an agile mind to easily flip between divergence and convergence. Likewise, researchers must develop this same agility to flip between qualitative and quantitative. Innovation expert and management theorist Roger Martin called this the "opposable mind," (Martin, 2007) and noted it is abductive logic (not deductive or inductive) that characterizes true innovators. Mixed methods researchers are a little like all kinds of innovators: they can think in different ways on command.

FIGURE 3: *The British Design Council's Double Diamond*
(Onarheim & Friis-Olivarius, 2013)

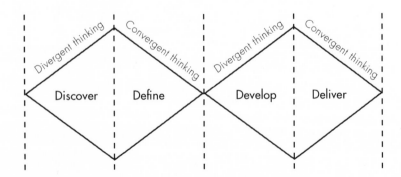

MITIGATING THE WEAKNESSES OF QUAL AND QUANT RESEARCH

It's tempting to become extra positivist when working as an applied qual researcher. Our stakeholders are unfamiliar with the constructivist perspective and ask only for scale and causation. However, given the coherence and customer focus of qual data, qual researchers should not simply shoehorn deductive methods onto inductive data. If you are a qualitative researcher, you should double down on the strengths the constructivist approach provides. Help your stakeholders luxuriate in the people they are making things for. Give them permission to fall in love with their customers. Show how participants come to believe a certain thing. Describe the workarounds they employ to complete certain tasks. Lay bare their thoughts, dreams, motivations and hidden beliefs that explain why they are not making so-called rational choices.

Qualitative researchers can augment this richness by sketching out some kind of scale and causation. How often did a particular workaround happen? You do not need to predict this incidence in the population at large, but you can at least show how often it happened in your study. Show causation in a different way: how people interact with objects, social structures and other people, and how they make decisions. Instead of zeroing on a single independent variable that causes an effect in a single dependent variable, qual researchers can paint a holistic picture of what forces affect any one thing to cause another thing. Hammersley (2014) suggests that qualitative researchers aim to describe causation in one of two ways:

1. Create plausible models of causation using imaginative tools like metaphors literary devices, and thought experiments to explain how a thing might work in many different contexts, in abstract language

2. Conduct a deep analysis of observed, empirical data to generate explanatory concepts that can later be tested quantitatively

In either case, causation will be *explained* if not firmly established within an acceptable confidence interval. Explanation is perhaps the most underrated strength of qualitative research! In this way, qual researchers can demonstrate the strengths of their approach and mitigate its weaknesses.

Likewise, quantitative researchers should also lean into the inherent strengths of their ontological position. Of course you should provide the quantitative data your stakeholders crave, like scale and causation. Tell them how many times a thing happened, to how many people. Prove or disprove hypotheses. Aspire to show causation experimentally, and most definitely zero in on the effects of independent variables on dependent variables. But at the same time, don't take social categories for granted. Offer some analysis of how something like "race," for example, can be nuanced and not simplistic. Do your best to tell good stories, perhaps with illustrative qualitative data like direct quotes.[5] Accept that you will not have deep detail in any one category and that your stakeholders will not enter the world of your participants. But at the very least, give them more than boring charts, graphs and numbers. Introduce some character and plot and attempt to paint a holistic picture.

If qual and quant researchers provide all the benefits of their primary approach, plus some of the benefits of their secondary approach, stakeholders will become sophisticated customers of research, and the entire organization will become more attuned to both the objectivist and constructivist approach. This is a key ingredient to innovation itself. Show me a company that balances customer focus with the pursuit of large-scale revenue targets, and I'll show you a very successful company. As Harvard Business School sociologist Rosabeth Moss Kanter notes, innovative companies fall in love with their customers and loosen strict goals for large-scale revenue, at least in the short term: "Not every innovation has to be a blockbuster," she writes, and "Tight controls strangle innovation" (Kanter, 2006, p. 79). Mixing qual and quant is spanning all the core competencies of innovation.

---

that proving something experimentally in a lab always extends to all other contexts. The problem with objectivism is not the belief that we can show causation, but that proving causation in a single instance is somehow proving causation in all instances (Potter & Lopez, 2001).

WHY MIX METHODS?

THERE SOME CLEAR REASONS WHY a researcher would choose to mix methods, most of which relates to the practical demands of a typical research project. Just like designers, researchers must respond to the real-world constraints of timelines, budgets and resources. Just like designers, they can use these constraints to inspire themselves to create innovative solutions (Borja De Mozota, 2003). Researchers should not fear these practical constraints but instead, use them as drivers of creative research solutions. The typical practical reasons why you might choose to mix methods include:

1. Time does not permit in-depth qualitative research

2. Time does not permit in-depth quantitative research

3. Negotiating access to participants is challenging

4. Finding a large data set is challenging

Surprisingly, these practical concerns affect both qual and quant approaches. Most applied researchers believe quantitative research is far quicker and less complex than qual, but in fact, great research of any sort typically takes time and resources, regardless of your ontological or epistemological starting point. Quantitative researchers may have ready access to data already collected (using the Census, for example) but oftentimes you will find that a great data set that focuses on your exact research question does not exist. Making good data takes time, whether it is qual or quant.

A great example of just how difficult it is to create great quant data sets is the recent paper by Oscar Jorda and his team at the Federal Reserve Bank of San Francisco (Jordà, Knoll, Kuvshinov, Schularick, & Taylor, 2017). They wanted to answer a straightforward question: is the rate of return on wages higher than the rate of return on forms of capital, such as real estate? It seems like a rather simple, straightforward question, based on a typical question any economist might ask. Yet Jorda and his colleagues could not find a single source of data available to answer this question. They had to combine two data sets (one on rents and another on house prices), which required a great deal of preparation and care before they even began analysis. In Jorda's case, he decided making the data set was worth the time. But you may not have the time and resources Jorda had. Instead, it might be worth exploring mixed methods if you find yourself with such practical limitations.

The conceptual reasons for mixing methods move beyond mere practicalities: you may have very specific research questions that beg for a mixed approach. In his summary of mixed methods, Bryman (2006) outlines five methodological reasons for mixing methods:

1. Complementarity: deepen or enhance other data

2. Expansion: expanding the inquiry to ask different questions

3. Development: use one method to inform and improve the other

4. Triangulation: corroboration of earlier data

5. Initiation: resolving earlier contradictory findings

In each one of these cases, a researcher chooses mixed methods to enhance their overall research findings, rather than simply responding to a practical problem like lack of time. Bryman notes, however, that most researchers who mix methods leave their reasons unstated. In his review of mixed methods literature, Bryman found a surprisingly large number of studies that did not mention why they chose to mix methods at all. Very few used "initiation," or attempted to understand why their previous findings were confusing or inconclusive (see Figure 4 below). He cautions strongly that researchers who do not state a methodological reason for mixing methods risk mixing for mixing's sake—and ultimately undermining the quality of the insights uncovered.

FIGURE 4: Why did researchers choose to mix methods?

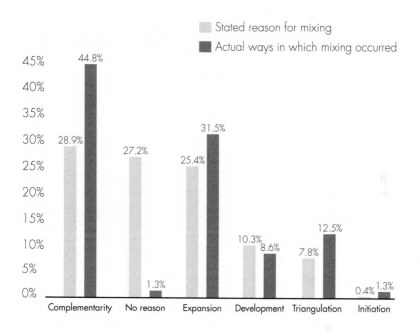

WAYS TO MIX METHODS

JUST AS YOU MIGHT EXPECT, there are multiple ways to mix research methods. Cresswell and Plano Clark (2007) provide a very succinct, 3-type model of the ways to mix methods, all of which focus on what you do with the data. In any of these three types, the research results are a product of both types of data, and by extension, a product of both types of philosophical assumptions. Note, however, that the way you mix implies a priority or dominance of one approach, and also implies a sequencing of events.

FIGURE 5: Cresswell and Plano Clark's 3-type Model of How to Mix Qual and Quant Data

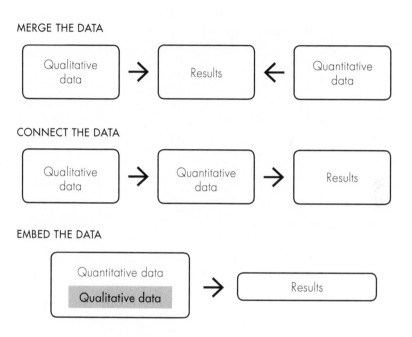

MERGE THE DATA

CONNECT THE DATA

EMBED THE DATA

In each of these cases, you are mixing both data types and philosophical assumptions, and each design has different impacts. Merging data is perhaps the most challenging because the conflicting belief systems themselves are merged, so you will need to consider this in the analysis and interpretation phase (as noted below, qual and quant perspectives have different ways of doing analysis and interpretation). Returning to the example of gender, imagine merging data from qualitative interviews about how people think about their own gender, and then quantitative survey results about how many people identify as which gender. Can you do inductive and deductive reasoning at the same time?

It might be easier to *embed* or *connect* the data, because this allows you to give prominence to one kind of logic (see Priority or dominance below for more detail).

Once you've discovered the practical and conceptual reasons to mix your methods, and you've done some initial thinking about whether you will merge, connect, or embed your data, it's time to start planning your mixed-methods study in earnest. This is not just a project plan, but a vision of what you would like to achieve. In the following sections, I provide a step-by-step approach for planning and executing a mixed-methods study in an applied setting. Unlike an academic textbook, I spend a great deal of time discussing the organizational context of doing this research, and how to manage the organizational challenges of doing research with and for stakeholders who are not well versed in research methodology.

HOW TO MIX METHODS, STEP BY STEP

As with any project, research projects benefit from starting with clear expectations. As I wrote in my book *Practical Ethnography*, managing the research project is about creating a shared sense of purpose and continually communicating that purpose to the wider team. Mixing methods also requires that you frame your objectives early. This involves understanding your stakeholders' needs and establishing a shared understanding about the choices and methodological and practical trade-offs the team has collectively agreed upon. As the project progresses, your general task is to steer the ship back toward that shared understanding. Stakeholders will ask for or even demand insights that you cannot deliver, but that is simply because they are not as familiar with the trade-offs inherent to mixing methods. If you continue to remind them of these trade-offs, stakeholders will begin to use your language toward the end of the project.

PROJECT KICK-OFF AND FRAMING

In this stage of the project, your goal is to give everyone a clear, shared understanding of what the project will achieve. This entails learning your stakeholders' needs, detailing the resources at your disposal, and then describing your approach to best meet those needs and resource constraints. Share the outcome of this process in the form of a shared artifact, either as a document or a diagram, and continually draw stakeholders' attention back to that shared understanding by using the artifact as a touchstone. As Stahl (2006) notes, shared artifacts are key to creating shared knowledge, particularly if that shared knowledge is a result of a negotiation process. The artifact itself becomes the symbol of the negotiated understanding about what the project is all about. This first step is especially important if the wider team of stakeholders is a relatively new team, or without a long history of working together. Shared beliefs and the artifacts that symbolize them are a key component to effective collaboration.

DEVELOPING SHARED UNDERSTANDING ABOUT RESEARCH NEEDS AND RESOURCE CONSTRAINTS

It is important to listen to what your stakeholders say they need, even if you know for a fact you cannot deliver their research wish list. It might seem like a waste of time to gather research requests that you cannot fulfill, but it serves a subtle and important purpose: you are engaging in a reciprocal dialog with your stakeholders. This reciprocal dynamic indicates that you are listening, considering and involving, but also advising and directing. Your stakeholders may be accustomed to issuing orders to research teams and may occasionally enjoy upbraiding them for not following them. Setting aside time for stakeholder needs disrupts this pattern and instead sets the tone as one of listening and responding as a consulting expert. Schedule time to listen to what they want, and then even more importantly, repeat that back to them in concrete ways. You can host a meeting in which stakeholders can individually list their unanswered research questions, and then capture each question in written form. Concretize that information by sharing the list with everyone so the entire organization knows how much is left to do. When I did this at a former role, I uncovered 116 unanswered research questions and made sure everyone knew how long that list was. It helped the team understand that they weren't the only ones with unanswered questions, and that the research team could only answer so many at one time. It also helps stakeholders understand how their individual piece of the product puzzle fits with other pieces.

Assign each research question to a person responsible for answering it. If possible, estimate how long it might take to answer each question, and it will quickly become clear how much of a backlog of work exists. This also lays bare how expectations may or may not be realistic in concrete ways. It may also reveal how under-resourced the research team is, and so may justify budgets to hire vendors or new, full-time researchers. Once the needs and resources are obvious, you will spend less time fighting off new research requests and more time prioritizing existing requests. I like to assume good intent with all stakeholders, that they simply do not know how much demand there is for research across the organization and systematically underestimate how much time it takes to complete any task. Showing them a baseline of what resources you have, and the demands on those resources, starts a productive conversation. Again, creating a shared artifact that communicates the needs and resources required will help significantly.

FRAMING YOUR APPROACH: INDUCTIVE OR DEDUCTIVE FRAME?

The unique value a researcher brings to an organization is her expertise in research methodology. Just like a chemist suggests a particular type of chemical analysis, or an engineer suggests a particular kind of mechanical solution, a researcher suggests a particular way to ask and answer questions. Research leaders should help stakeholders understand the nature of asking deductive or inductive questions, the trade-offs each represent, and some strategies to mitigate any shortcomings of choosing one approach over the other.

Return to your list of unanswered questions. Which of those are inductive and which are deductive? Help your stakeholders understand the outcomes of any particular approach. They honestly may not know that deductive reasoning will result in narrow results, or that inductive reasoning will yield durable insights, useful beyond a single study. Your expertise as a researcher needs to be in the room when decisions about which frame to use are being asked.

Deductive questions are typically very narrow and, frankly, somewhat counter-intuitive. It is common for stakeholders to start with beliefs about a topic and to call them "hypotheses," but to stop short of developing actual, specific hypotheses such as "H1: women employees are more satisfied than men employees." Routinely, we see examples more like, "I don't know what we'll find but I think there might be some difference between men and women's satisfaction." While it's completely acceptable to have beliefs instead of hypotheses, a deductive approach requires a crisp, falsifiable statement. Help your stakeholders sharpen their deductive questions into falsifiable statements, which can then be proven true or false. Don't let people off the hook. If they want to establish scale and causation, they have to follow the scientific method.

A purely deductive study will start with a clear and falsifiable hypothesis such as "women employees are more satisfied than men employees," and then would prove or disprove that assertion. A deductive approach begins with a reason to believe a certain thing is going on, either through prior research or through theory, and you set out to test whether that is true. In the employee satisfaction example, you may have surveys from prior years that demonstrate women are more satisfied than men, you may have already done interviews that seem to indicate that pattern, or perhaps you have read a theory that predicts women being more satisfied than men. Regardless, you have reason to believe it to be true, and a deductive study would specifically state you are setting out to disprove this assertion. You collect some data that asks about gender and satisfaction and run a test for significance to see if the men and women's responses differ significantly. As it turns out, women are significantly more likely to agree with the statement, "It is satisfying working at this company." And there it is—deductive study is thus concluded. You were unable to falsify your hypothesis, so therefore it is true.

By contrast, an inductive study will start with very open-ended questions like, "What is going on in our organization? How are employees feeling? What are their concerns, if any?" Such a study seeks to understand, "What is important?" As Van Maanen writes, qualitative research is "procedures for counting to 1" (Van Maanen, Manning, & Miller, 1986). In other words, inductive studies seek to understand what counts. Unlike a deductive study, an inductive study does not set out to falsify a belief. A lot of stakeholders are surprised to learn they are not actually "scientific" (aka positivist) in their approach because they have much more exploratory needs. In the ideal inductive approach, you will not have any prior beliefs about gender and its effects. In Strauss and Corbin's famous description, "The researcher begins with an area of study and allows the theory to emerge from the data" (Strauss, A., & Corbin, 1998, p. 12). This is grounded theory, or theory that is grounded in the data that are collected. You can see how this inductive approach is squarely focused on the participants themselves.

In your inductive study, you might find out that women tend to talk differently about the workplace than men do, and you wonder what this difference indicates. You dig deeper in the data, and realize that women see the organization as a "family," while men see it as a transactional place where you simply "do business." So, there is a gendered pattern in these beliefs. You also discover that men and women have very different ways of interacting with coworkers. Women interact with coworkers outside work with fitness classes, book clubs and informal play-date circles with their kids. Men have little to no outside-work interactions with co-workers, and even mention that being a man means being more "business like," or less socially inclined with co-workers.

So, you conclude that women make sense of the organization differently because of this very dense and interconnected social network full of coworkers, and feel free to do so because it is gender-appropriate. Men, on the other hand, feel it is gender-inappropriate to establish social ties with co-workers, which has the negative downstream effect of them feeling isolated, alone and ultimately less satisfied with work than women. In the end, the data tell you the general, explanatory patterns of gendered experience at work.

Making the choice between an inductive or deductive approach is much easier than making the choice to merging these two approaches. The opposing logics of deductive and inductive inquiry complicate everything: research design, method, analysis and interpretation. As Cresswell (2011) tells us, quantitative research will measure pervasiveness of things we already know, and qualitative research will uncover things we don't know much about. He writes:

> Mixed methods research, then, is more than simply collecting qualitative data from interviews, or collecting multiple forms of qualitative evidence (e.g., observations and interviews) or multiple types of quantitative evidence (e.g., surveys and diagnostic tests). It involves the intentional collection of both quantitative and qualitative data and the combination of the strengths of each to answer research question (J. Cresswell et al., 2011, p. 5)

When you map your inductive and deductive questions, be aware you are potentially merging different ways of thinking and different types of logic. For this reason, it's also useful to prepare your stakeholders for this as well, so there is absolute clarity about what mixing data sets implies. If the group all agrees that inductive and deductive approaches are both required, merging your data implies a complexity that requires a high degree of sophistication on the part of both the researcher and the consumers of the research. This might be ultimately worth it, but it is not for the faint of heart. Some teams are not ready to approach this challenge. Organizational culture research tells us there are additional, social aspects to successful research projects, which I explore in the next section.

SOCIAL INFRASTRUCTURE: PREPARING TEAMS FOR MIXED METHODS

Organizational psychologist Amy Edmondson argues in her influential work on psychological safety[6] (2018) that volatility,

[6] Some may recognize this phrase as what was used in Google's noted Project Aristotle (Duhigg, 2016), conducted by the People Analytics team. In this project, Google researchers set out to discover what differentiates successful teams. They had no pre-conceived idea of what that meant, but interestingly, they chose a deductive method to determine the answer. They used quantitative data from many sources and sifted through the data to find the right combination. Nothing stuck. They could not disprove a single hypothesis. They had no clear correlations with anything—until they discovered Edmondson's concept of psychological safety. It turns out, Project Aristotle is a good example of a *deductive method* being inappropriately applied to an inductive question: what makes teams successful? Had the researchers started with a literature review, instead of with quantitative data, they

uncertainty, complexity and ambiguity (VUCA) are hallmarks of the modern organization. VUCA organizations move quickly, and often must make decisions with incomplete information. In VUCA organizations, Edmondson argues, psychological safety is an especially important antecedent to productive collaboration. Groups need have a shared belief that being wrong is not grounds for dismissal, but the natural outcome of trying new things. While it's certainly not desirable to be wrong, it should be reasonably expected, from time to time, that learning implies being wrong. Smoothly functioning organizations have just such a foundation.

You might call this foundation a kind of social infrastructure. Just as research teams require technical and intellectual infrastructure of software tools and methodological skills, they also require a social infrastructure of psychological safety. Sadly, research is often asked for precisely when the organization is grappling with volatility, uncertainty, complexity and ambiguity. This makes it all the more important that the social infrastructure is secure before any research (and potentially troubling insights) comes to the fore. Your role as a research leader, therefore, is to engender a climate of psychological safety, to prepare your stakeholders to have realistic expectations, and to act as promulgator of those shared beliefs. Preparing your stakeholders de-risks the research project. It will improve your team's ability to make decisions quickly and under pressure— exactly when you'll need it.

---

would have had better luck uncovering these key attributes of successful teams. Instead, they rooted around in quantitative data as if it were rich qualitative interview transcripts, using a grounded theory approach to what was actually a hypothesis-appropriate data set.

Build this social infrastructure by managing stakeholder expectations. All too often, stakeholders believe research projects will *guarantee success* of a product or service, instead of simply *learning about* a product or service. To mitigate this, gather the team together and facilitate a discussion about the philosophical tensions inherent to the mixed-method approach. It may sound a little overwrought to create a meeting titled, "Research Project Sync: Potential Philosophical Divisions," so instead, just consider this an opportunity to advise stakeholders of potential expected outcomes.

To be specific, your job in such a meeting is to ensure people understand that mixing types of data sometimes becomes confusing because it also implies different schools of thought and different ways of looking at the same information. In addition, communicate that there is no such thing as failure if your only goal is to learn. Once everyone realizes that the goal of research is simply to learn, and that most definitely is a guaranteed outcome, you will have more room to maneuver in if your findings.

Some strategies to manage expectations include creating hypothetical findings and interactively mapping them according to the type of finding, the usefulness of such a finding, and the likelihood of being able to actually uncover such a finding. Imagine having several dozen hypothetical findings printed on index cards and asking stakeholders to place each finding along a spectrum of "useful" to "not useful." They can also discuss how each finding might make them feel, or what implications it might have. For example, if you were to find that some men were very angry at being held to unacceptably high expectations about long hours in the workplace, is that a useful finding? How likely is it that we would learn this in our research? What is the first-blush, emotional reaction to such a finding? What might we do with this finding? Having such dry-run experiences will prepare your stakeholders for the reactions they might have, which could range from "That can't be true!" to "I knew it all along!" to even, "That's completely useless information." Guide your stakeholders to a realistic expectation of what is possible to prove in an inductive approach, and what is possible to understand deeply in a deductive approach.

This kind of meeting is best done in person, if possible, with an interactive session that produces physical artifacts that show stakeholders about the areas of overlap and potential tension. For example, sorting sticky notes of research questions onto a spectrum from deductive to inductive on a white board will show where the likely areas of tension might arise. If it's not possible to host an in-person meeting, "gathering the team" can mean a focused teleconference that also produces artifacts that show this same spectrum. Overall, the group should know which direction they lean towards — inductive or deductive — and understand the trade-offs of that choice. Regardless of how you organize this gathering, the key is to produce a shared understanding that choosing mixed methods has practical and philosophical concerns, but ultimately yields better results.

Producing a shared artifact is key to ensuring a shared belief about this process. Written documents are fine to generate, though in some organizations, documents do not fit neatly into typical knowledge structures. Word documents or even Power Point documents often require focused, individual attention to be fully absorbed. If you have even an ounce of doubt of whether this is the case in your organization, opt instead for a diagram to summarize the complete, negotiated shared understanding the team has.

While it would be ideal for every member of the extended team to read and fully digest a document, it is often not the way knowledge is shared in contemporary organizations. If you must write a document, consider adding a diagram to the document that can serve as a shorter summary. Diagrams like Indi Young's mental model (Young, 2008) or affinity maps (Maher, Hadfield, Hutchings, & Eyto, 2018) or even simple mind-mapping diagrams that are loosely organized thought bubbles that represent the goals and objectives discussed by the group. Whatever type of artifact you decide on, ensure that it's easily accessible to everyone and is regularly seen without anyone having to put in much effort to look for it. Refer to it often in communications and meetings. It will become the thing that reminds your stakeholders that they cannot have everything, and in fact, they already agreed to compromise.

With this meeting, you will make the team think, which is a small miracle in today's typical corporation. In their fantastic (and depressing) book, *The Stupidity Paradox*, sociologists Alvesson and Spicer examine the apparent widespread epidemic of stupidity in companies today. They write, "Functional stupidity is the inclination to reduce one's scope of thinking and focus only on the narrow, technical aspects of the job. You do the job correctly, without reflecting on purpose or the wider context" (Alvesson & Spicer, 2016, p. 24). Any meeting focusing solely on expectations challenges functional stupidity because you are asking people to think broadly. You need to acknowledge that this makes people uncomfortable and give them the permission to think. Setting aside time for the luxury of thinking will grease the wheels of collaboration and make future action go so much more quickly. Clear understanding is the core of concerted action. As philosopher Martha Nussbaum tells us, understanding is not a luxury but a very practical concern: "Understanding is always practical, since without it action is bound to be unfocused and ad hoc" (Nussbaum, 2018, p. 12). Clear and shared understanding is the core of collaboration. Groups that share beliefs (some might call this "culture" for short) have been shown to be more productive and less conflict ridden, even when they are geographically distributed (Fuller, Hardin, & Davison, 2007).

The social infrastructure of psychological safety, shared beliefs, and shared artifacts create a solid foundation for research design. Researchers with a strong social infrastructure will have more leeway to ask adventurous questions. Over time, they will have a bank of political capital that will underwrite research questions whose value may only be unlocked years or even decades in the future.

You may take several cycles to build this infrastructure. Maybe it will take you three or four research projects before you convince your stakeholders to think broadly, or to map potential findings according to inductive/deductive logic or usefulness. Maybe they will fight you when you ask them to think. But do not give up. Your courage and confidence as a research leader will inspire them to slow down and spend just a few precious moments thinking about the implications of their actions. If you persevere, you will earn not only their respect, but also the coveted and rare outcome of building a thinking organization.

RESEARCH DESIGN

In the research design phase of the project, your fundamental goal is set yourself up to make analysis and reporting as straightforward as possible. It implies making choices that will generate data that are of particular shapes and sizes, so you need to think two or even three steps ahead. This would be true of any research study, but it's even more challenging to do when mixing methods: you need to imagine how your collection activities shape the data in both qual and quant ways.

In quantitative studies, research design is typically painstaking because at this phase, researchers must consider every possible hiccup in data collection, because you cannot change the design during collection. Quant researchers take great pains to structure the knowledge before any data are generated, and analysis is relatively straightforward once the data are gathered.

In qual studies, by contrast, research design is open-ended, looser and more able to cope with change. The key difference is that qualitative researchers structure the knowledge after data are collected. If you describe this process using the double diamond of design, quant research design is convergent, zeroing in on specific things, while qual is divergent, being more open and exploratory. Qualitative research design may look a little loosey-goosey, but it is actually quite purposeful. Skilled qualitative researchers know how to balance the need for agility and change along with gathering data in a way that will still yield insights. Skilled mixed methods researchers design studies that are both convergent and divergent. They know what must be written in stone before data collection and what can be adjusted as the project unfolds.

Mixed methods research design should prioritize the most important questions of stakeholders, whether they are inductive or deductive. Since you have already recorded and deprecated the less-important research questions, the research design document should not become the object of a struggle. Instead, the research design is specifically crafted to answer a specific question and will not be a boundary object that serves as a proxy for the "but you didn't listen to me" complaint. The research design should also clearly emphasize inductive or deductive approaches, the sequencing of the data collection activities, as well as the concepts you intend to focus on (for the qual portion of the study) and the specific variables you will measure (for the quant portion of the study).

PRIORITY OR DOMINANCE

The extended stakeholder group should be very clear on which approach is going to be dominant: inductive or deductive. Mixed designs include both, but one will always take precedence over the other. An inductive-dominant research design will have a constructivist perspective, so it will assume that participants are making sense of something. The overall goal of the study is to interpret that process. A deductive-dominant research design will have an objectivist perspective, so it will assume there is a given set of facts, and the study's objective is to uncover those facts by means of proving or disproving a hypothesis.

Returning to our example of gendered experiences in the workplace, an inductive-dominant approach will not take "gender" as a given category but will instead see it as a role that employees make sense of and negotiate. Interviews, focus groups, contextual inquiry, ethnography or even narrative analysis will provide researchers with data that reveal what "being a man at this company" is all about.

Researchers may uncover that "being a man at this company" is fraught with anxiety and contradiction. Men are expected to be strong and to perform with excellence, but to do so they must ask for help from collaborators and supporters. They must choose between appearing strong and asking for the help they need. They risk appearing weak on the one hand, and overworked and isolated on the other. You decide to augment this understanding scale and causation: how pervasive is men's anxiety, and how is it connected to their ability to ask for help? What other variables (e.g. age, tenure) might affect this anxiety? You may do a survey to understand scale and causation.

If you decide on a deductive-prominent approach, you will start with clearer assumptions and specific hypotheses. You take gender for granted in this approach and perhaps hypothesize that women are less satisfied than men. You have reason to believe this because you know fewer women are in leadership positions. You survey men and women about their satisfaction levels and discover that it's actually men who are less satisfied, not women. You're not entirely sure why, so you conduct focus groups to find out why your hypothesis was not borne out by the quant data. You learn that leadership positions are themselves challenging for anyone—man or woman—without adequate support systems in place. You learn that women are more satisfied for two general reasons: they rationally assess that leadership roles may require more support, so they either opt out with full awareness of what they are doing, or they pursue leadership because they have better support systems in the first place. Women's conception of the workplace as a "family" helps them in unexpected ways, you may conclude, so perhaps men too could benefit from finding family-like connections with co-workers, whether through fitness classes, or book clubs, or whatever other social groups the men are interested in forming.

Whatever dominance you choose, be clear about what this means for your results. In an inductive-dominant approach, you are focusing first on that luxurious understanding of your subject matter. You are stepping back and then diving into The Encounter. You may not have a great grasp on scale or causation, but you will have deep understanding. If you choose a deductive-dominant approach, you will focus first scale and causation of what causes what. You may come up short in your pursuit to luxuriate in the customer, and you might not have the deepest understanding of your context. But you will be able to count the incidence of a thing and test what affects what. In either case, prepare your stakeholders—and yourself—for what you will and will not have.

DATA COLLECTION: SIMULTANEOUS OR SEQUENTIAL

Mixing methods means mixing data types, but it also means organizing different kinds of activities. As noted above in Figure 5 (see page 37): Cresswell and Plano Clark's 3-type Model of How to Mix Qual and Quant Data, how you decide to mix your data actually implies a sequencing. In other words, mixing data has very practical concerns: what do you do first? In our gender in the workplace research design example, we assumed that a sequential design is the right design. In our inductive example, we explored how employees understood gender first, and then moved to establish scale and causation (Cresswell and Plano Clark would call this an example of "connecting the data"). In our deductive example, we first tested a prior belief, and became a little puzzled at the outcome, so moved onto a more inductive method to solve the paradox. But you can also play with timing of certain activities (this is also an example of connecting the data). Simultaneous designs (qual and quant at the same time) will give you a lot of data in a short period of time, which can cover scale and causation, and coherence and participant focus. Sequential designs are more challenging because they take longer, but they also provide more of a careful approach, and ultimately a deeper understanding. We don't always have the time for sequential designs and it's not necessarily better to stagger your data collection. Don't be afraid to tackle simultaneous designs, which result in large amounts of data all at once, and consider tackling sequential designs, which result in longer time horizons, and require a more abstract vision of what you're trying to answer.

SEQUENTIAL DESIGNS

Sequential designs take longer than simultaneous designs, so we often dismiss them out of hand in applied settings as having unrealistic timelines or being impossible to execute. Yet, if you consider every successive research project you complete as just one phase in a long-term, sequential research design, it begins to seem more possible. Instead of thinking two to three months out, consider thinking two to three years out. Is it possible to answer all your inductive and deductive research questions over three years? Probably. You may also find that if you implicitly stitch together all your research projects, you have probably already conducted many mixed-methods studies, just without the concerted plan of doing so.

Every research study can become a sequential design— *eventually.* As my students at the Ontario College of Art and Design University (OCADU) can attest, I love to tell researchers that they are secret agents inside their organizations. It's unlikely that a senior executive will green-light a three-year, sequential research plan, arguing it will take too long, be too expensive and won't provide immediate insight. If only every applied researcher just smiled and nodded, and said, "Sure, boss," and did what turns out to be phase one of the study immediately, and slowly but surely over the next three years, conducts each sequential phase of the project. In three years, this researcher will produce a comprehensive knowledge base that answers hundreds of research questions using both constructivist and objectivist ontologies, positivist and interpretivist epistemologies, deductive and inductive logic, and ultimately provides scale, causation, coherence and a participant focus. That would change everything.

Not all sequential designs are truly mixed methods— you can do quant-only or qual-only sequential designs. That is perfectly acceptable if your needs are more deductive, or inductive respectively. After your initial research design phase, it may make complete sense to use only quant methods or only qual methods. Whatever you decide, make sure you and your stakeholders know what you are giving up.

TABLE 2: *Types of Sequential Research Designs*

Design	Example	Best suited for	Constraints
Qual → Quant	Ethnography plus survey	Inductive-dominant approach to explore first then measure or test	Need to adequate time to analyze equal data before creating quant variables
Quant → Qual	Survey plus focus groups	Deductive-dominant approach to establish scale then zero in on something specific for more detail	Need time to analyze survey results
Quant → Quant	Census-like survey followed by shorter follow-up survey with smaller sample	Deductive-only approach that collects general baseline data and connects those to more specific variables	Not a mix; no induction; no coherence or participant focus
Qual → Qual	Foundational ethnography followed by follow-up interviews	Inductive approach exploring generally and then exploring one particular topic more deeply	Not a mix; no deduction; no scale or causation

SIMULTANEOUS DESIGNS

If you have determined that there is simply no time or no need to use a sequential design, a simultaneous design is a potential alternative. It's obviously not optimal to do more work at the same time, unless perhaps you have a qual specialist and a qual specialist available at the same time. It's rare that a single person is capable of the sheer workload of doing two methods at the same time but it is certainly possible. If you are planning on doing this yourself, prepare to switch contexts and modes of thinking. It's not impossible to do, but it does require a thoughtful and purposeful switch from inductive to deductive, perhaps even in the same day. For example, you may decide to analyze customer Web traffic on your company's website, in addition to interviewing a small sample of participant customers. You need to approach the analytics data with a deductive mindset, and form hypotheses that are falsifiable. But you also need to approach the interviews with an inductive mindset, and explore how participants understand your company's product. It's possible to do, but it does require some agility in thinking style.

TABLE 3: *Types of Simultaneous Research Designs*

Design	Example	Best suited for	Constraints
Qual + Quant	Interview plus analytics	Inductive-dominant to compare beliefs (interview) against actual behaviors	Possible to uncover contradictions that may require deep analysis
Quant + other Quant	Survey and analytics	Deductive-dominant to compare beliefs (survey) with behavior (analytics)	Likely to find contradictions; no induction to explore why
Qual + other Qual	Ethnography and focus groups	Inductive-dominant to compare context with beliefs at some scale	Focus groups provide some scale but not a deductive approach

CLARIFYING CONCEPTS OR VARIABLES

During the research design phase, it's also critical that you have a more specific idea of what you are investigating. Even with the most inductive approach, it is still useful to have a crisp understanding of what you are looking for before you begin gathering data. In his famous essay "What's Wrong With Social Theory?" sociologist Herbert Blumer argued that clear concepts are essential to researching the human world. He called them "sensitizing concepts," or concepts that lend themselves to areas that are begging for investigation. If you call it "sex," you may not be looking for ways in which gender is performed or architected. But if you use the concept of "gender," you will likely see instances where people feel compelled to police themselves back into a defined box of masculinity. For example, if you follow Judith Butler's concept of gender, you will assume it to be a kind of performance, or "drag," as she puts it (see for example Butler, 1999). This leaves the door open for you to learn from your participants what they believe their gender to be. Gender is a theatrical approximation that people are continually acting out. Given this definition, you will not waste time wondering if the way your participants talk about their cars or their wardrobes is really a proxy for gender; you will have a clear understanding that these are props they recruit to express gender and not gender itself. If you start with the concept of "sex," it will not sensitize you to this role-playing nature.

Whatever you are researching, write out clear conceptual definitions for the major areas of concern. What, for example, is "employee experience"? Don't take it for granted but take the time to clarify what it refers so. From there, you can operationalize the concept by describing how it can be recognized in data. This might be a description of the qualities of employee experience, but it might also be specific variables if you are studying it quantitatively. Employee experience may refer to the "emotional, physical and material experiences an employee has while working, and while thinking about working."

Once you have clear, sensitizing concepts, you set yourself up to save a lot of time during the analysis phase. In her wonderful study of nurses solving problems, Tucker (2004) found that most operational failures in hospital wards could be traced to breakdowns in the supply of materials or information inside the hospital. She also found that nurses compensated quickly for these breakdowns, using their own manual workaround strategies. It was Tucker's precise conceptual definition about what caused a failure that led her to the bigger insight: nurses did not control the processes that generated breakdowns and obscured their existence because of their quick workarounds.

DATA ANALYSIS AND INTERPRETATION: MIXING INDUCTION AND DEDUCTION

Every researcher struggles with answering the question "so what?" You found out that men's concept of their gender makes it harder for them to connect to their coworkers. So what? You discover that customers hate the new interface, even though they can complete their tasks faster. So what? It's the most difficult question to answer because it means leaning strongly toward coherence and participant focus, and away from causation and scale. Understanding the big picture is an inductive task. It is incredibly difficult because it means going out on a limb and saying, "this is what this is all about," without necessarily having the specific, tiny insights that deductive approaches give us. It's always easier to disprove a single fact than it is to describe a complete system. But when you mix methods, you must do both.

Describing complete systems requires inductive data analysis and interpretation. Many non-researchers are familiar with the term "data analysis," but few people are familiar with the concept of interpretation, or the process whereby the researcher *explains* the data. Your goal in data analysis is to organize the data so that it may easily answer the research questions you've already shared with the wider team. Your goal in interpretation is to provide additional contextual insight about the data. Data analysis is actually a very mechanical process. Contrary to popular belief, it does not involve magic or fairy dust; it is a very straightforward set of steps for both qualitative and quantitative research. Many people know quantitative data analysis activities such as calculating measures of central tendency like average, or measures of dispersion like standard deviation. Those untrained in qualitative data analysis are often surprised to learn that it too is quite rigorous and has specific, mechanical steps. The bad news is that qualitative data are, by definition, less structured than quantitative, and therefore require more mechanical work to whip into shape.

In their well-known text on qualitative data analysis, Miles, Huberman, and Saldana (2014) outline a very straightforward three-step process:

1. Reduce the data

2. Visualize the data

3. Draw conclusions and verify with the data

It is step number 1 that trips up most novice qualitative researchers, partly because they are accustomed to quantitative data, which is far easier to reduce. You can collect all the quant data at once, and reduce it quickly and easily. By contrast, qual data can easily become too voluminous and unwieldy unless it is reduced at every step of the research process. Reduction in quant data is summarizing using, for example, the average of a particular variable. But what is "average" in qual data? As Finnish cultural theorist Pertti Alasuutari (1995) notes, there is no such thing as a "typical" case in qualitative research—every case is unique. This makes it a lot harder to mechanically organize your data into easy summaries, like summary statistics.

Qualitative, inductive analysis is not trying to reduce data to a summary using averages or frequency tables, but to reduce in another way: to describe the phenomenon in abstract, explanatory ways. This is difficult because it involves understanding–and confidently stating–the essential drivers of change in the given area you are studying. This is less like summarizing and more akin to solving riddles. As Alasuutari writes, "In other words, when using qualitative analysis as a means to explain or make sense of a phenomenon we do not use as evidence the frequencies with which something occurs together with another. Instead, riddle-solving provides a good analogy of the type of reasoning employed" (Alasuutari, 1995, p. 7).

Inductive analysis involves unriddling, sensemaking, looking at the big picture, or explaining. In this sense, qual data analysis is harder than quant because it necessarily involves interpretation. A researcher can simply state average income, or average height of their quant study sample, and get away without saying anything about what it means. But qual researchers cannot do that. They must interpret as a function of analysis, which goes beyond just listing observations. As Susan Spiggle's (1994) fantastic article on qual data analysis notes, interpreting qual data is not the same as analyzing it. Analysis, for Spiggle, is performing specific actions on the data, while interpretation is something deeper and more creative. You can start with categorizing beliefs or actions of participants, for example, to complete your analysis, but to *interpret* those actions, you need to unriddle them, or elevate their meaning. It takes a great deal of skill to explain complex social phenomena simply and elegantly, but also with abstract, explanatory power. Step 2 of Miles, Huberman, and Saldana's model involves using various visualization techniques (e.g., diagramming, summary tables like conceptual matrices), and then using that visualization to start making assertions and drawing conclusions. Inductive reasoning is grounded in the data, as Strauss and Corbin (1998) remind us in their work on grounded theory. As you move onto Step 3, ensure you have evidence to support your claims, and to further reduce those data down to simple but powerful explanatory statements.

An example of this kind of abstraction process is Latour and Woolgar's (1979) study on how scientists work. Latour and Woolgar observed scientists closely and documented their specific activities, such as writing papers or using mass spectrometers. Instead of simply reporting this usage in frequency or detail, Latour and Woolgar go further and imagine what the act of using the mass spectrometer symbolized. Scientists would take physical specimens and put them into the machine to map their contents. After they did this, they could generate charts and graphs, and more symbolically "manufacture scientific facts," in Latour and Woolgar's explanation. The act of feeding scientific instruments with physical specimens was the act of making an ethereal thing called a "fact." The new fact was still nascent and a tiny baby fact, and did not become a fully grown-up fact until it was published in a scientific journal. This is the symbolic nature of doing science, they argued: scientists use instruments to create facts and write scientific papers to promulgate them as real. This is what Spiggle means when she says that "Abstraction... surpasses categorization in that it collapses more empirically grounded categories into higher-order conceptual constructs" (Spiggle, 1994, p. 493). Induction goes beyond "this is what we empirically observed" and uses symbolic tools like metaphor to describe the deeper meaning of a given set of behaviors.

You can see how difficult it is, then, to mix inductive analysis with deductive analysis. Deduction involves starting with a general theory or set of beliefs, and using that as a starting point to interpret a specific case. Induction is the opposite: it starts with a specific case (say, when a scientist puts a specimen into a mass spectrometer) and then makes a general statement about the nature of science, for example. The challenge most researchers have with induction is that it appears to be "bias." Even using the word "creative" to describe the interpretation process may raise eyebrows as evidence of bias. When people say "bias," they really mean the researcher will not accurately predict future outcomes or the results of particular changes in independent variables (for example, if a respondent's income is higher, will they be more likely to purchase this product?). But as Spiggle notes, inductive approaches must, by definition, involve creativity. You cannot explain a general phenomenon without breaking out of established concepts because you are actually developing new concepts. Spiggle explains, "...interpretation occurs as a gestalt shift and represents a synthetic, holistic and illuminating grasp of meaning, as in deciphering a code" (Spiggle, 1994, p. 497). Unfortunately, developing new concepts will by definition defy reliability because it is breaking new ground.

Just like in the research design phase, the analysis phase requires a mixing not just of data, but different schools of thought and different procedures. When you mix deductive and inductive reasoning you are first testing and falsifying prior beliefs, and second, unriddling or abstracting, and coming up with new explanatory concepts.

When you take qual data and attempt to falsify prior beliefs, this is where the dreaded "How many people did you talk to?" question comes from. Stakeholders believe that large sample sizes determine validity (they don't), and also believe, however unconsciously, that falsification is the goal of all research. Novice researchers often attempt to make their qual data somehow more "scientific" by making their sample sizes larger, or by using frequency tables or summary statistics to describe their data. However, it's a failure in waiting because qual data do not support falsification and can never rise to that standard.

Instead of forcing deductive logic onto inductive data, try to use the logics in the right ways. Of course you should use summary statistics to summarize quick insights from your very small sample, but stop short of attempting to falsify a prior belief. For example, in a study on medical errors, researchers used their qualitative codes of types of errors and counted them to show the kinds of errors that were occurring. Note their sample size was nine hospitals and they made no attempt to falsify or prove causation (see Table 4: Typology of Medical Errors in Nine Hospitals below). Instead, they unriddled what they observed, and created a new set of concepts around types of errors. Inductive interpretation involves providing models, diagrams and concepts to describe how and in what way a system works. Provide typologies to give people an understanding of the various ways things work. In other words, participant focus and coherence are your goals.

Adding deductive data and logic to this process means going back toward causation and scale as your twin goals. If you complement your qual data with some quant research such as a survey, do not use verbatim comments in a comment box to unriddle what's "really going on." Leave that logic for the rich data provided in interviews of ethnographic observation. Instead, use the survey to do what surveys do best: asking large numbers of people the same question (Lecompte & Shensul, 1999). Test which variables affect other variables and get larger sample sizes to test known patterns. Avoid shoehorning survey data to give you a "why" or "in what ways" of your topic. Focus on what causes what, and by how much. When using both methods together, you should have solved a riddle for your stakeholders and falsified (or failed to falsify) some prior belief.

TABLE 4: *Typology of Medical Errors in Nine Hospitals (Tucker, 2004)*

Hospital	Type of hospital	# of beds	Nursing units observed	Unionized nurses	Observation time (hr:min)	% of total observation hours	# of nurses interviewed
1	Small community	47	Intensive care unit	Non union	82:35	34	0
2	Specialty, urban, teaching	98	Surgical	Non union	7:45	3	0
3	Rural community	134	Medical/ surgical	Union	27:19	11	2
4	Community, private not-for-profit	243	Surgical and maternity	Non union	34:30	14	1
5	Community, government	292	Oncology and medical/ surgical	Union	15:35	7	3
6	Community, government	250	Cardiac	Union	1:30	1	1
7	Teaching, urban	198	Oncology	Non union	20:30	9	2
8	Pediatric, teaching, urban	163	Oncology	Union	9:11	4	1
9	Teaching, tertiary care	433	Intensive care unit	Non union	40:30	17	2
					Total: 239:25		13

CAN ANALYSIS AND INTERPRETATION BE A TEAM SPORT?

Often in applied settings, you will see researchers gather their stakeholders to do "group synthesis sessions." The goal of such sessions is for stakeholders to internalize, adopt and hopefully advocate for the major insights from the study. This is a laudable goal, to be sure, but it is not a great strategy to gather untrained people, for a finite amount of time, and perform surgery on precious participant data. Participants trust you to treat their words and experiences with care and thought. Bringing together 12 people who are not trained in doing so and asking them to interpret the data is inefficient at best, and disrespectful at worst. Instead of using synthesis sessions as the primary way to interpret data, consider using these sessions to introduce sensitizing concepts that will have a life beyond this single study. Use these sessions also to perform some of the more mechanical tasks of analysis (that is, to chunk the data into categories or into a spectrum of gravity). But it is still the researcher's responsibility to guide the overall interpretation of the data, primarily using past research and theory as a guide. Researchers must always be able to answer "So what?" because they have been trained in intellectual concepts and ideas that help answer that question. Non-researchers do not have this background, and should not be counted on to treat participants' data with the skilled touch it deserves.

I will typically organize such sessions with a clear set of sensitizing concepts. Returning to the example of gender and employee experience, I might start the session by introducing the idea that gender is a role that people adopt and not a variable that determines their behavior. I might then ask the group to look for examples in the data of employees adopting, rejecting, or otherwise grappling with the normative role their gender suggests. This approach treats the participants' data with care and respect, but also elevates the discussion. The group will have a better understanding as to why some act in expected ways and others do not. They will likely begin to question the objectivist conception of gender as determinant, and as a bonus, begin to think about paradoxes. It's not realistic to expect everyone to become sophisticated data analysts in a single session, but over time, with sufficient exposure to sensitizing concepts, stakeholders can become better pattern recognizers.

DURING REPORTING

Once you have integrated deductive and inductive data analysis and interpretation, reporting should be somewhat obvious and straightforward. You have mechanically organized your data into usable chunks that you can now slice and dice and put into a report. This should be true for both inductive and deductive data. But the chunks you choose and how you present them will differ, depending on the data type. Remember, if you have a mixed methods project, your goal is to show coherence and participant focus on the one hand, and causation and scale on the other. You are aiming to take the best of inductive and deductive reports and merge them. In your research design phase, you prioritized which approach was dominant and communicated that to your stakeholders. This priority will be mirrored in your report.

If your design was inductive-dominant, your report at a minimum should focus clearly on participants and give stakeholders a coherent understanding of what you're researching. To make it a great mixed-methods report, you should also include some sense of scale and causation. This means choosing qual data that will reveal participants as full humans, with needs, pain, joy and contradiction. Intuitively, many researchers know that video clips of participants seem to move their stakeholders. But keep in mind that if you don't do this with care, you run the risk of using participants as props in your own agenda, and not actually taking the participant's perspective. Strive to be purposeful here, instead of just intuitive.

Think through the kinds of stories that will grab stakeholders' attention, but also that tell a story that is complemented by the quant data, following Bryman's description of complementarity. Let's say you're studying working experiences and gender, and you're trying to tell the story of how many men feel alienated from their co-workers. You have some quant data that starts telling that story, and you should have some qual data that make those dry numbers come alive. It's especially helpful if the qual data provide a sense of coherence, as well as the emotional mindset of participants. Consider selecting quotes that feature participants trying to grapple with paradoxical or ambiguous situations. One participant may tell you he recognizes it's not good for him to keep his work relationships superficial, and that he should cultivate a sense of comradery with his coworkers, but he doesn't seem to know how, and it bothers him. This will give more detail to the statistic: "64% of men at this company feel their relationships with coworkers are not deep." The quote pushes stakeholders to see more than just the statistic, and the counterintuitive nature of the story conveys the complexity of the issue. It's not as simple as "men think their relationships at work aren't deep." Look for ways to explain the complexity, using participants' own words to paint the complete picture.

Try to avoid the temptation to use qual data to manipulate your stakeholders to adopt your own personal agenda. I personally have been guilty of simply allowing very compelling participant stories to move what I have considered important. I have told myself in the past that my agenda is righteous and good, and therefore using emotion-laden video clips is totally justifiable. It's not. Today, I work hard to avoid doing that because my agenda is *not my participants' agenda*. They don't care about a particular product and its future. Their paycheck doesn't rely on my desire to have a VP change her mind about something. Participants have different concerns than I do. I work hard to bring *their concerns* to the top of my list. As you prepare your report, ask yourself, "Is this something a participant would say is important, or is just what I think is important?"

This is not to say that you must report what participants say, verbatim, without contextualizing their views within the wider system in which they work or live. There may be reasons to highlight something that is invisible to participants, but that you have seen and identified as a key driver to the overall functioning of that system. After all, one of the hallmarks of ethnography is the ability to describe the entire system, based on the views of individuals *within that system* who may not see its whole form. A truck driver who drives consumer goods to a distribution center may not know anything about the experience of shipping those goods across the ocean, and just because he doesn't talk about that doesn't mean it's not important. But if he talks about time pressure and lack of sleep, the researcher's job is to connect that experience to what they learn about the shipping schedules, the expense of adding extra days to the ocean-leg of the journey, and how it connects to the truck driver's perceptions. The job of qual data is to tell participants' stories and to describe the system as a whole.

The inductive-dominant report should offer explanations of how systems work, by using things like typologies of customers, or models of how a thing occurs (such as a customer journey), or the complex inter-relationships between people and things. In the academic world, researchers tend to rely on long, text-based descriptions of such a system. A wonderful example of this kind of lyrical writing can be found in Clifford Geertz's (2000) famous comparison of a wink versus a mere tick of the eye.[7] In today's corporate environment, it's unlikely that teams will spend time reading blocks of such text, no matter how well written it is. So in order to complement the text-based description, inductive reports can include diagrams and visualizations that describe the typologies or models. It helps here to have at least a small design sense. Better yet, involving designers allows them to first deeply understand the data and second to think through representing it in a way that others can well understand. I have lost count how many times I've read a wonderful academic study, marred by incomplete, incomprehensible, or just plain ugly diagrams.

---

[7] In this description, Geertz summarizes a key point made originally by Gilbert Ryle, that is, humans know the difference between a wink and just an inadvertent blink because of the layers of meaning on top of the deliberate movement. There is a wink, which is discernible to most humans, and then there is an exaggerated wink, which implies a parody of the original wink. This is where Geertz famously described his "think description" for the first time.

If you find yourself hesitating because you doubt your design ability, consider recruiting a designer, or better yet, take some information design courses. It has been my privilege to work with some of the best designers in the technology industry, who taught me hierarchy, color, typography and composition.[8] I don't pretend to be as good as they are (not even close!) but I have learned that good enough design is not out of reach for me. I just need to focus on the meaning the diagram conveys.

Even better than diagrams are metaphors. Using cohering metaphors provides stakeholders with a deep understanding of a thing, without the temptation to ask for deductive logic. Using our gender in the workplace example, you could describe gender in several metaphorical ways, and use illustrative stories and quotes to provide further detail. "Gender as cloak" might be one that explains how both men and women "hide" behind their gender to avoid confronting something they don't wish to deal with. Men may avoid the issue of caring work by saying something like, "You know how we men are; we just don't know how to take care of people." Women may avoid having hard conversations by saying something like, "Women just aren't good at being confrontational." In both cases, men and women are using their normative gender role as a "cloak" to hide from unpleasant experiences.

[8] Once upon a time, I trained as a journalist. We were required to take a newspaper layout class, which, at the time, I considered boring and complete waste of my time. To this day, I remember the basic principles of choosing a "lead story" and highlighting it "above the fold" of my report. If you want to get inspiration for great content layout, take a look at the front page of a top newspaper. You will see immediately which story is the most important (at least according to the editors).

In their wonderful book on doing anthropological research, Denny and Sunderland suggest asking a simple question in inductive reporting: "What is 'X'?" Coffee, literally, is a hot brown liquid, they note, but metaphorically, coffee is a social lubricant, or a morning ritual, or a business tool. Metaphorical language is a good way to explain the hidden, social complexities of a thing and its cultural meaning. It has the added benefit of being easy to understand. It's surprising how often stakeholders find themselves gaining deep understanding with metaphors, and somehow forgetting to ask deductive questions about hypotheses.

Deductive-dominant reports disprove hypotheses, following Popper's guidance on falsifiability. A mixed-method report should, at a minimum, offer a sense of scale and causation. Starting with scale, provide your stakeholders with a detailed numerical accounting of some portions of whatever you are studying. This can (and probably should) stop short of very precise measures, usually because the typical mixed-methods study is unlikely to have an advanced way of measuring sensitizing concepts or variables. Stakeholders should come away from a mixed-methods report knowing how big a thing is, in general terms, and what mechanisms are at play in terms of causation. You do not need to have precision measures of scale, nor do you have to prove definitively the cause of one thing. But your stakeholders should know generally how big your qual findings are, and potentially what is causing what.

It's instructive here to understand what makes a purely deductive report. A purely quantitative social science study might focus on a concept that is very well known, and has been studied quantitatively for decades, but perhaps not in this particular way. A recent example is the research by Anne Case and her partner Angus Deaton (2015) in their paper on American life expectancy. Certainly, life expectancy studies have been done for many decades, but Case and Deaton zeroed in on types of deaths such as drug overdoses, suicides and cirrhosis of the liver—what they called "deaths of despair"—and coupled them with inability to work due to disability or chronic pain. Together, these measures provided a novel insight into American life, while using a very well-known concept. The main challenge Case and Deaton confronted was the *complexity of measurement* and the specifics of causation. But they had absolutely zero in the way of qual data, and they spent many years developing a precise and elegantly beautiful data set. This the highest bar for quant studies; your mixed methods study need not meet this bar.

In your mixed-methods report, the deductive portion will give a sense of how big a phenomenon is, and what might be causing what. Unlike Case and Deaton, you do not need to create an innovative new measure of an abstract concept, nor do you have to prove definitively what causes what. You just need to give a sense of scale, and a reasonable, educated belief of what causes what. This can be achieved rather simply by using frequency tables. The nursing study of hospital errors (see above) is a good example of establishing both a sense of scale and causation. The researchers counted the size of the hospital, how many nurses they employed, the time spent with participants, and categorical variables like whether it was a unionized or non-unionized hospital. They don't claim to say how much a hospital's size affects error rates, but they do give a sense of patterns, which could then be tested more specifically in a deductive-only study.

Deductive elements of your report do not need to establish falsifiability definitively. But they should give a sense of what you might find, should you do a quant study, focusing on those specific questions alone. We tend to overestimate the importance of such findings, however, and truly underestimate the power of inductive reasoning. After all, without a coherent understanding of a system, and how participants of that system think and feel, it's unlikely you will be able to intervene effectively to fix that system. It's tempting to focus on firmly establishing causation on a single variable, and while that can be valuable, it's far more important to have a basic, scientific understanding of how a system functions. You cannot skip that step; why would you want to?

Overall, the goal of mixed-methods reporting is to provide more insight than just an inductive or deductive report alone. You have chosen a dominant approach and should stay true to that in your report, but you need not match the level of excellence that other social scientists might achieve in their qual or quant-only studies.

NEW HORIZONS FOR MIXED METHODS RESEARCH

It's an extraordinary time for the automated collection of quantitative data. Once upon a time, all quant data had to be created manually through surveys or painstaking observations of human behavior. Now, our devices and software create endless reams of what Davis and Davidson (1991) dubbed "data exhaust," or the data that are automatically generated through digital interactions. This is incredibly exciting for researchers because we now have access into human behavior through a passively collected, empirical method. But I often tell people to tamp down their excitement about data exhaust because none of these data are actually designed for falsifiability in mind—it's simply the detritus of our digital lives. Just because we have more data doesn't mean we are doing better research. We are drowning in an endless sea of data, yet we are stuck in an insight desert. Such is the contemporary experience of many researchers.

Data exhaust includes meaningful events like the number of times a person logs into a website, or less meaningful events, such as the number of times a user's computer pings a server (whether at a human's direction or not). Web analytics are the best-known example of data exhaust, and designers have used these data to great effect. As I explained in *The Handbook of Log File Analysis* (Ladner, 2008), web analytics were born out of old-school log-file analysis, which was invented by and for website administrators who wished to monitor server loads on their websites. It was never designed to be a data-collection method, much less a bona fide social research method like surveys or structured interviews. Web analytics data today are problematic for two reasons. First, they do not measure intentionality on the part of the user. Just because a computer records a click does not mean that a human intended to make that click. Second, web analytics require a great deal of non-standardized interpretations on the part of the analyst, making one analyst's interpretation wildly different from another's because of their differing beliefs about what "counts" even when analyzing the exact same data set. Anyone who has spent time with the raw data generated by analytics tools will attest to this challenge.

More data are not necessarily better. A person's social media profile, plus their passively collected web-traffic data, plus their daily interaction with their smartphone will equal a potential goldmine of insight but also an enormous data set. Market research company Statista estimates that the average individual will have 1,429 digital interactions with others per day by 2020, growing to 4,909 by 2025. But this is just for a single user. Even adding another 29 users (30 is often considered the minimum number of cases to be used to draw statistical inference), would generate a completely unusable amount of data on just a single day. It's becoming rapidly apparent to analysts that "data science" is more about formatting troublesome data than it is about answering meaningful questions. Data science as a discipline is not one that focuses on a subject area, like human-computer interaction or even online consumer behavior, but more on the tools and techniques of data management (such as SQL, Python and R). The sheer volume of data means data scientists spend much of their time creating data sets *so that they might be able to ask questions* rather than spending all their time asking challenging or innovative research questions.

It cannot be denied that we have the potential for more deductive reasoning than ever before. We just have to whip data exhaust into actual data. How might we do that? The challenge is not to create more data, but to be purposeful and strategic in choosing (or better yet, creating) the data that are most likely to be easily falsified. One of the key ways to take advantage of data exhaust is to intervene with a researcher's eye early on in the development of a digital product that might yield data exhaust, and to turn mere exhaust into falsifiable data. A marketing team might be designing a digital advertising campaign. A researcher could intervene and set up a falsifiable statement such as, "People who saw this ad purchased the product" as a guide for metrics in the digital ad. Or an apparel company might be preparing a new spring collection, with a branded, umbrella name such as "Spring to Work." A researcher could intervene and create a falsifiable statement such as "People who receive the Spring to Work email are more likely to purchase from the new collection." This too could lead to a code snippet in the online store. In this approach, there is an implicit focus on both scale and causation. We assume people who see an ad are affected by it. The research skills remain the same: great research identifies clear concepts, operationalizes them into variables, and then uses an elegant data set to determine causation.

If crafting falsifiable data is not possible, then you can use the concept of falsifiability to help you prioritize which data exhaust is likely to yield the most insight. For example, look at how the data exhaust is created: is it primarily about load balancing a server or some other, back-office type event? If it is, it's much easier to make a falsifiable statement whether the server is overloaded than whether a user finds their desired outcome. Likewise, when looking at digital interactions on a smartphone, many of the interactions passively recorded relate to connectivity and stability of the system, and not about user experience per se. Consider first data that relate to a user's success: ability to log on within one second instead of number of times logged in, in a single day. Some of these data will not be readily available off-the-shelf, so consider writing falsifiable statements before writing a single line of SQL code to extract digital interactions. Here are some examples of falsifiable statements relating to human behavior and digital devices:

- Users send a message to a fellow user within three minutes of signing up (relies on specific, discrete interactions that can be recorded in a single user session).

- Customers open the app multiple times a day (can be derived from user IDs and time stamps).

Here are some examples of statements that are much harder to falsify because they imply mixing two sources of data:

- Users who get five friends in the first session or more are more likely to be satisfied (mixes an empirical observation of getting friends with an opinion that must be completed with a survey).

- Customers open the app multiple times a day in order to find something they left in their cart (also mixes empirical data with subjective belief, which would come from an interview).

In general, using data exhaust is more challenging than people initially estimate. Your first job is to wrangle the data exhaust into falsifiable statements, and only then attempt to mix the data with subjective perceptions from surveys or from interviews. Make it easy on yourself and work prioritize data that can most quickly be turned into falsifiable statements about human behavior. The main issue to keep in mind is that empirical data is not always better, and is almost always more complex to collect than first believed.

CONCLUSION:
TO MIX OR NOT TO MIX?

IT NEVER CEASES TO AMAZE me how bottomless the practice of social research can be. I've practiced research for almost 20 years and I still find myself noticing tiny nuances in technique that I had never noticed before. What happens if you try asking a survey question with a yes/no binary choice online instead of in-person? What happens if you wear different clothes to the usability lab? How do participants react when you sit beside them instead of in front of them? What if you force participants to use physical objects to numerically rate their experience? What if you don't write a single interview question at all, and just sit and listen? There are endless ways to push your craft, and endless ways to become a better researcher.

My journey started in the qualitative, interpretive camp. I learned how to make sense of qual data before I began mixing it with quant data. Others may start with quant and move toward qual. Regardless, each researcher has their own ontological and epistemological position, even if they don't know it. I started my research journey with an objectivist point of view that I had learned in high-school chemistry class, even if I didn't know it at the time. My scientific training made it challenging for me to understand the interpretivist method. It was tempting to dismiss interpretivist research as "subjective" or "biased," but I learned that kind of lazy thinking is really unproductive. Likewise, it's easy to dismiss objectivist research as bland, simplistic, or reductionist. But that too is taking the easy way out. If you are curious about mixed methods, you owe it yourself to think deeply about your own perspective and interrogate it. This challenge will give you a deeper insight. As F. Scott Fitzgerald once wrote, "the test of a first-rate intelligence is the ability to hold two opposed ideas in the mind at the same time, and still retain the ability to function. One should, for example, be able to see that things are hopeless and yet be determined to make them otherwise." (Fitzgerald, 1936, p. 69). So too it should be with applied research; let us struggle day to day with our stakeholders demands for quant data, and work tirelessly to mix it with qual.

REFERENCES

Ader, L. N. (2011). *Ethnography as theory. HAU: Journal of Ethnographic Theory*, 1(1), 211–219.

Alasuutari, P. (1995). *Researching Culture: Qualitative Methods and Cultural Studies.* Thousand Oaks, CA: Sage.

Alvesson, M., & Spicer, A. (2016). *The Stupidity Paradox: The Power and Pitfalls Of Stupidity At Work.* London: Profile Books.

Anderson, K., Nafus, D., Rattenbury, T., & Aipperspach, R. (2009). Numbers Have Qualities Too: Experiences with Ethno-Mining. In *Ethnographic Praxis in Industry Conference Proceedings* (pp. 123–140).

Bearman, P. S., & Stovel, K. (2000). Becoming a Nazi: A model for narrative networks. *Poetics, 27*(2–3), 69–90. https://doi.org/10.1016/S0304-422X(99)00022-4

Berger, P., & Luckman, T. *The Social Construction of Reality* (1966). New York: Anchor Books.

Borja De Mozota, B. (2003). *Design Management: Using Design to Build Value and Corporate Innovation.* New York: All Worth Press.

Bryman, A. (2006). Integrating Quantitative and Qualitative Research: How Is It Done? *Qualitative Research, 6*(1), 97–113. https://doi.org/10.1177/1468794106058877

Bryman, A., & Teevan, J. (2005). *Social Research Methods: Canadian Edition.* Don Mills: Oxford University Press.

Butler, J. (1999). Imitation and Gender Insubordination. In C. Lemert (Ed.), *Social Theory: The Multicultural and Classic Readings* (pp. 575–585). Boulder, CO: Westview Press.

Case, A., & Deaton, A. (2015). Rising morbidity and mortality in midlife among white non-Hispanic Americans in the 21st century. *Proceedings of the National Academy of Sciences, 112*(49), 15078–15083. https://doi.org/10.1073/pnas.1518393112

Crabtree, A., Rodden, T., Tolmie, P., & Button, G. (2009). Ethnography considered harmful. In *Proceedings of the 27th international conference on Human factors in computing systems - CHI 09* (p. 879). New York, New York, USA: ACM Press. https://doi org/10.1145/1518701.1518835

Cresswell, J., Klassen, A. C., Plano Clark, V., & Clegg Smith, K. (2011). Best practices for mixed methods research in the health sciences. https://doi.org/10.1002/cdq.12009.

Cresswell, J. W. (1994). *Research Design: Qualitative and Quantitative Approaches*. Thousand Oaks, CA: Sage.

Cresswell, J. W., & Plano Clark, V. L. (2007). *Designing And Conducting Mixed Methods Research*. Thousand Oaks, CA: Sage.

Davis, S., & Davidson, B. (1991). *2020 Vision: Transform Your Business Today To Succeed in Tomorrow's Economy*. New York, NY, NY: Simon & Schuster.

Denzin, N., & Lincoln, Y. (2000). Introduction: The Discipline and Practice of Qualitative Research. In N. Denzin & Y. Lincoln (Eds.), *Handbook of Qualitative Research* (2nd ed., pp. 1–30). Thousand Oaks: Sage.

Duhigg, C. (2016, February). What Google Learned From Its Quest to Build the Perfect Team. *The New York Times Magazine*. Retrieved from https://www.nytimes.com/2016/02/28/magazine/what-google-learned-from-its-quest-to-build-the-perfect-team.html

Edmondson, A. C. (2018). *The Fearless Organization: Creating Psychological Safety in the Workplace for Learning, Innovation, and Growth*. New York, NY: Wiley.

Fitzgerald, F. S. (1936). *The Crack-up.* New York, NY: New Directions Books.

Fuller, M. a., Hardin, A. M., & Davison, R. M. (2007). Efficacy in Technology-Mediated Distributed Teams. *Journal of Management Information Systems,* *23*(3), 209–235. https://doi.org/10.2753/MIS0742-1222230308

Geertz, C. (2000). *The Interpretation of Cultures.* New York: Basic Books.

Hammersley, M. (2014). *The Limits of Social Science: Causal Explanation and Value Relevance.* Los Angeles: Sage.

Jordà, Ò., Knoll, K., Kuvshinov, D., Schularick, M., & Taylor, A. M. (2017). *The Rate of Return on Everything, 1870–2015* (Working Paper Series No. 24112). Washington, DC. https://doi.org/10.3386/w24112

Kanter, R. M. (2006). Innovation : The Classic Traps. *Harvard Business Review,* (November), 73.

Ladner, S. (2008). Watching the Web: An Ontological and Epistemological Critique of Web-Traffic Measurement. In J. Jansen, A. Spink, & I. Taksa (Eds.), *Handbook of Log File Analysis.* (pp. 64–78). Hershey: Information Science Reference (IGI Global).

Ladner, S. (2014). *Practical Ethnography: A Guide to Doing Ethnography in The Private Sector.* Thousand Oaks, CA: Left Coast Press.

Ladner, S. (2015). Managing the Private Sector Research Project. In R. Dingwall & M. Byrne McDonnell (Eds.), *Sage Handbook of Research Management* (pp. 307–320). London; Thousand Oaks, Calif.: Sage.

Latour, B., & Woolgar, S. (1979). *Laboratory Life: The Social Construction of Scientific Facts.* Beverly Hills: Sage.

Lecompte, M., & Shensul, J. (1999). *Designing and Conducting Ethnographic Research.* Walnut Creek: Altamira Press.

Lipo, C. P., Hunt, T. L., & Haoa, S. R. (2013). The 'walking' megalithic statues (moai) of Easter Island. *Journal of Archaeological Science, 40*(6), 2859–2866. https://doi.org/https://doi.org/10.1016/j.jas.2012.09.029

Maher, C., Hadfield, M., Hutchings, M., & Eyto, A. De. (2018). Ensuring Rigor in Qualitative Data Analysis : A Design Research Approach to Coding Combining NVivo With Traditional Material Methods. *International Journal of Qualitative Methods, 17*, 1–13. https://doi.org/10.1177/1609406918786362

Martin, R. L. (2007). *The Opposable Mind.* Cambridge, MA: Harvard Business School Press.

May, R. (1994). *The Courage to Create.* New York: WW Norton.

Miles, M. B., Huberman, A. M., & Saldana, J. (2014). *Qualitative Data Analysis: A Methods Sourcebook. Third Edition. The SAGE Handbook of Applied Social Research Methods.*

Narayan, K. (2012). *Alive In The Writing: Crafting Ethnography In The Company Of Chekhov.* Chicago, IL: University of Chicago Press.

Nussbaum, M. (2018). *The Monarchy of Fear: A Philosopher Looks at Our Political Crisis.* New York, NY: Simon & Schuster.

Onarheim, B., & Friis-Olivarius, M. (2013). Applying the neuroscience of creativity to creativity training. *Frontiers in Human Neuroscience, 7*, 656. https://doi.org/10.3389/fnhum.2013.00656

Pinch, T., & Bijker, W. (1984). The Social Construction of Facts or Artefacts: Or How the Sociology of Science and the Sociology of Technology Might Benefit Each Other. *Social Studies of Science, 14*(3), 399–441.

Popper, K. (1962). *Conjectures and refutations: The growth of scientific knowledge.* New York, NY: Basic Books.

Potter, G., & Lopez, J. (2001). General Introduction: After Postmodernism: the Millennium. In J. Lopez & G. Potter (Eds.), *After Postmodernism: An Introduction to Critical Realism.* London: Athlone Press.

Small, M. L. (2011). How to Conduct a Mixed Methods Study: Recent Trends in a Rapidly Growing Literature. *Annual Review of Sociology*, *37*, 57–86. https://doi.org/10.1146/annurev.soc.012809.102657

Spiggle, S. (1994). Analysis and Interpretation of Qualitative Data in Consumer Research. *Journal of Consumer Research, 21*(December), 491–504.

Stahl, G. (2006). *Group Cognition: Computer Support for Building Collaborative Knowledge*. Cambridge: MIT Press.

Steiner, C. (1999). Constructive Science and Technology Studies: On the Path to Being? *Social Studies of Science, 29*(4), 583–616.

Strauss, A., & Corbin, J. (1998). *Basics of Qualitative Research* (2nd ed.). Newbury Park, CA: Sage.

The British Design Council. (2015). The Design Process: What is the Double Diamond? *Design Council*. https://doi.org/10.1038/sj.ijo.0801425

Tucker, A. L. (2004). The impact of operational failures on hospital nurses and their patients. *Journal of Operations Management, 22*(2), 151–169. https://doi.org/10.1016/j.jom.2003.12.006

Van Maanen, J., Manning, P., & Miller, M. (1986). Editors' Introduction. (J. Van Maanen, P. Manning, & M. Miller, Eds.), *Sage University Paper Series on Qualitative Research Methods* (Vol. 1). Beverly Hills, CA: Sage.

Young, I. (2008). *Mental Models: Aligning Design Strategy with Human Behavior*. New York, N.Y.: Rosenfeld Media.

Yuan, Y., Major-Girardin, J., & Brown, S. (2018). Storytelling Is Intrinsically Mentalistic: A Functional Magnetic Resonance Imaging Study of Narrative Production across Modalities. *Journal of Cognitive Neuroscience, 30*(9), 1298–1314. https://doi.org/10.1162/jocn_a_01294

ABOUT THE AUTHOR

Sam Ladner is the author of *Practical Ethnography: A Guide to Doing Ethnography in The Private Sector.* She is a sociologist who studies technology use, particularly in the workplace, and has published widely on applied research methods. She has worked at major technology companies including Microsoft and Amazon, and currently works as a Principal Researcher at Workday. She also teaches applied research methods through the Ethnographic Praxis in Industry Conference (EPIC) organization. She holds a PhD in sociology from York University in Toronto, and lives in the San Francisco Bay Area with her husband and cat.

Made in the USA
Middletown, DE
12 February 2020